D1796649

How to Avoid Employment Tribunals

How to Avoid Employment Tribunals

And What to Do if You Can't

Colin Everson

Gower

© Colin Everson 2002

The materials that appear in this book, other than those quoted from prior sources, may be reproduced for education/training activities. There is no requirement to obtain special permission for such uses.

This permission statement is limited to reproduction of materials for educational or training events. Systematic or large-scale reproduction or distribution – or inclusion of items in publication for sale – may be carried out only with prior written permission from the publishers.

Published by
Gower Publishing Limited
Gower House
Croft Road
Aldershot
Hants GU11 3HR
England

Gower Publishing Company
131 Main Street
Burlington VT 05401-5600 USA

Colin Everson has asserted his right under the Copyright, Designs and Patents Act 1988 to be identified as the author of this work.

British Library Cataloguing in Publication Data

Everson, Colin
    How to avoid employment tribunals: and what to do if you can't
    1. Arbitration, Industrial – Law and legislation – Great
    Britain
    I. Title
    344.4'1'01133

ISBN 0 566 08433 3

Library of Congress Cataloging-in-Publication Data

Everson, Colin.
    How to avoid employment tribunals: and what to do if you can't/Colin Everson.
      p. cm
    Includes bibliographical references.
    ISBN 0-566-08433-3
    1. Discrimination in employment – Law and legislation – United States – Popular works.
    2. Employees – Dismissal of – Law and legislation – United States – Popular works. 3. Discrimination in employment – Problems, exercises, etc. 4. Employees – Dismissal of – Problems, exercises, etc. I. Title.

KF3464.Z9 E93 2001
344.7301'133--dc21   2001040541

Typeset in Plantin Light and Helvetica by IML Typographers, Birkenhead, Merseyside.
Printed in Great Britain by MPG Books Ltd., Bodmin, Cornwall.

Contents

How to use this resource

Welcome to this training resource, which is designed to help you handle the events both during – and most vitally preceding – an employment tribunal.

WHAT THIS RESOURCE IS – AND IS NOT – INTENDED TO DO

This resource is not intended to make you an expert on employment law. Given the complexity of the law, its rapid development and the effect of precedents flowing from case law on subsequent decisions, it is difficult for anyone to be an 'expert' in the subject on more than a day-to-day basis. Rather, it is written chiefly from the point of view of a 'fair-minded' employer,

- who tries to foster a good climate in the workplace
- whose formal grievance and disciplinary procedures do not need to be invoked frequently
- who intends to fight only inevitable legal battles that they can be confident of winning.

This should be the case in organizations both large and small, privately and publicly owned, unionized and non-unionized.

Fairness at work

All employees have a right to be treated fairly – you expect such treatment yourself when you are an employee, so why should lower standards apply to people who work for you? Promoting a climate that is fair and just to all employees will prevent most difficult – and potentially expensive – cases arising. This work is not intended to help you sack, dismiss, get rid of, let go – whatever the term in use may be – an employee, however unfairly they may have been treated. In any case, tribunals are staffed by people with a combination of legal training and industrial or commercial experience, who are very likely to see through a case that does not have real merit. 'Going to tribunal' is often expensive, always time-consuming, and frequently unnecessary if the right working relationships have been fostered throughout the organization.

ELEMENTS OF THIS RESOURCE

A variety of elements is provided. You can choose to use any or all of them in the way that suits your situation best. A brief description and suggested way of using each of them follows here. No model programme is given, as the exact needs can vary so widely among users of the materials. However you decide to use the resource, it should help you to ensure that:

- attitudes and procedures in your organization, whatever its size, are fair and can be proved to be so
- should the worst happen – and facing an employment tribunal is a costly and stressful worst case scenario for most people – you can face the proceedings knowing that you have acted fairly and in accordance with employment law to the best of your abilities and knowledge.

Read systematically through the entire resource, noting topics as you go that require action either directly, or through other people in your organization. A Personal Action List is provided within the Appendix, on which you can make notes as you read.

Introduction

The introductory section provides some straightforward background information on the subject of employment practices and legislation that affects them.

The risk management approach to employment tribunals

Risk management approaches are just as relevant to employment issues as they are to health and safety, product integrity, information security and insurance. Being taken to tribunals by employees, especially if this happens frequently and/or leads to costly awards to appellants, reflects on management attitudes and practices just as do high levels of accidents, frequent product recalls or leaks of sensitive information to competitors.

'Where there's blame, there lies a claim'

The title for Section 3 is deliberately suggestive of the general attitude of mind that prevails in modern society, exemplified by a host of commercials on TV and radio. This chapter gives some background information about the rising numbers of claims being made in the increasingly compensation-conscious culture with which organizations must cope. It describes the importance of case law, which to some extent makes the standard required of employers a 'moving target'. Actual examples of cases that reached tribunal, were withdrawn by the appellant, or were settled out of court are quoted, covering the major areas of unfair dismissal, race discrimination and sex discrimination. Also included are some cases that the appellant lost.

You may find the size of some awards made, or the grounds on which some of them were made, surprising or even shocking. Nevertheless, you must deal with the world as it is and build the potential costs of losing at a tribunal into your risk management strategy. Remember that the tribunal is not concerned with your ability to pay any compensation awarded. The sums are decided by standard formulae related to the losses that an appellant has suffered, including injury to his or her feelings in matters of race or sex discrimination.

Examples of some employment practices in recruitment and staff appraisal are cited, where they may prejudice or assist your case.

Personal attitude questionnaire

Use the personal questionnaire at least twice, firstly, as soon as you have read the introduction that follows this resource guide, then again after you have used any of the main case study materials, to check your attitude towards fairness at work.

The case studies

The three Case Studies are the kernel of this resource. They are all based on real-life situations and set in a variety of backgrounds, as summarized:

No.	Setting	Grounds for complaint	Representing appellant	Representing respondent
1	'SME' sector, manufacturing, wholesaling and retail business Non-union environment Partnership	Unfair Dismissal on the pretext of Gross Misconduct	Citizens' Advice Bureau	'Friend' of the respondent
2	Local branch of national distribution company Unionized environment sLimited company	Constructive Dismissal and Racial Discrimination	Amalgamated Trade Union and the Commission for Racial Equality	Solicitor retained by the company
3	Independent 'high tech' company, formerly part of larger group No union involved Limited company	Unfair Dismissal and Sex Discrimination	Equal Opportunities Commission	Solicitor retained by the company

Please read through the Case Studies carefully, focusing on those that are most nearly relevant to your own situation. First, select one of the Case Studies – for example, the one on sex discrimination – if you believe that this could become an issue in your organization. Then, use the Personal Attitude Questionnaire to test the temperature of your attitude and those of your working colleagues to employees in your organization.

Construct a training programme to suit the message that you need to spread through your organization, incorporating role-plays to help employees see other people's points of view. If you decide to run a formal programme, you will find suggested break points and topics for discussions throughout the Case Studies, which should also help if you are using the resource on a self- study basis. Finally, to use this resource to the best advantage:

- Use the Procedural Checklist on page 61 to see how well your procedures might stand up before a tribunal – if they have to.
- Set up a role-play for one of the Case Studies. Sufficient information is given in each of them to establish the characters involved and the situations encountered.
- Go on then to role-play your own situation if that is appropriate to your circumstances. Build in the tests shown under the Tribunal procedures chapter to test your attitudes and procedures before they are put to the ultimate test in court.

Procedural checklist

The Procedural Checklist has been cross-referenced to Case Study 1, dealing with unfair dismissal. It also has blank columns to enable you to use it as a check on your own procedures, dealing with issues such as handling grievances from employees, disciplinary matters, basic communications, training and supervisory approaches. A blank copy of the checklist is provided in the Appendices, for you to copy and use as required.

Tribunal procedures

This section is placed quite deliberately towards the end in the belief that a user of this training resource should seldom need to appear before a tribunal. However, if you do, it is as well to have an idea of what the tribunal members will be looking for, particularly in respect of the formal testing procedure they will apply to the case.

- If you 'role play' a case in which you know you will be involved, you can use the tests provided for each main category of appeal to challenge your own procedures and attitudes as they are likely to appear to a tribunal member
- It is much better to know in advance if there are significant weaknesses in your case
- Testing your own procedures and likely 'perceived attitudes' in advance is a prudent aspect of the risk management approach to employment matters advocated in this resource.

Glossary

A Glossary is provided, covering the likely key words, abbreviations and topics with which you need to be familiar. Examples are given where this is likely to be helpful. Some words are unique to employment tribunals, or have special or specific meanings from the legal point of view. It is essential, therefore, that you understand the vocabulary used if you are to face a tribunal, especially if you are representing yourself.

Appendices

Copies of a Personal Questionnaire, Procedural Checklist and Action Lists are provided for copying and using as often as you find appropriate.

Introduction: Handling employment tribunals effectively

The most effective way to handle employment tribunals, known until 1998 as industrial tribunals, is never to find yourself in front of one

● unless you are absolutely sure that your case will succeed.

To be confident of success, you will need to know, first, that

● you have behaved fairly and, second, be able to
● prove that you have done so.

The first of these requirements stems from your attitude and that of any other staff who may be involved in the case. The second will usually require written proof from copies of documents like Contracts of Employment, witness statements and records of disciplinary hearings and appeals.

The price of wrong attitudes, inadequate systems and procedures

Large organizations often retain expensive lawyers simply as a safety net to catch them when their systems and attitudes to people fail.

● They could save money by ensuring that their practices and procedures are fair and in good shape to begin with.

Smaller organizations frequently expect to lose if an employee claims that he or she was unfairly dismissed – the employer knows that their systems are inadequate, even if they believe that they have behaved fairly. They cannot afford to retain lawyers to plead a 'hopeless' case, so they offer to settle out of court, contributing to the thousands of cases settled in this way in just one year. That is frequently an unnecessary cost to the organization, as it usually far outweighs the cost of implementing simple, documented systems and making sure that all managers and employees behave fairly.

- with fair attitudes backed by simple, documented systems, many small to medium enterprises (SMEs) could see their former employees joining the ranks of applicants who withdrew their applications in the same year; much cheaper than settling out of court – or in court.

Employee responsibilities

Employees have duties, too, enforced by laws such as the Health and Safety at Work Act and the Food Safety Act. They, too, have contractual obligations under their Contract of Employment with their employer – assuming of course that they have one. All employees can be required to behave reasonably towards their colleagues, managers, customers, and with company property and confidential information – indeed to anyone and with anything they come into contact with in their daily work.

- However, disciplinary procedures need to be in place to cope with the minority of employees who cannot, or will not, accept their responsibilities to people, property and procedures, however thoroughly they have been trained, supervised and briefed.
- Remember always that the main role of disciplinary procedures is to encourage employees to improve – before the ultimate sanction of dismissal is imposed.

THE LAW

An increasing amount of legislation and case law affects how employers and employees must behave towards each other. One of the most basic legal requirements for an employer is that they must issue a written Contract of Employment and Terms and Conditions of Employment within two months of an employee starting work.

The small to medium enterprise (SME)

The vast majority of organizations are in the SME sector. For the very smallest, employing twenty people or less, this requirement does not apply. Nevertheless, there will still be an implied contract between the two parties, covering basic points such as rates and mode of pay, hours of work, holiday entitlement, disciplinary codes and how to express grievances.

Ignorance of the law

This is no defence under English law. A moment's thought will show why this has to be so. Look at these statements and imagine them put forward in court as a defence against charges brought to court:

'I didn't know there was a 30 mph speed limit on that road', 'I've never heard of the Health and Safety at Work Act' 'What is the Data Protection Act?'.

It would just be too easy for anyone accused of anything to claim 'I didn't know what I did was illegal' – and that includes employees as well as employers.

Seeking advice on employment law

Employment law is so complex that no one could reasonably expect an employer to be an expert in every aspect of it. If you believe you might be affected by the law over, say, the possible employment of a disabled person, the best course is to check what your legal obligations are before making a decision.

● This need not involve paying a lawyer, because if you do not have access to professional advice within your organization, ACAS, the local CAB or any trade association you may belong to should be able to help and their advice will be free, or virtually free.
● It is worth remembering that the cost of not taking this advice could be tens of thousands of pounds in extreme cases. When you are facing the risk of such crippling financial losses, ignorance is definitely not bliss.

Verbal contracts

In law, a verbal contract is as valid as a written one. However, in practice, it can be said with justification that: 'a verbal contract isn't worth the paper it's not written on'. Although that is not technically correct under the law, it is much harder to enforce a contract for which there is no written evidence. Once you are before a tribunal with many thousands of pounds in compensation at stake, there is a good chance that memories will fail – yours and the applicant's.

● Once you are in the situation of pitting one person's (uncorroborated) word against another's, there is no telling which party the tribunal may believe.

The risk is too great to take. It makes sound financial sense for all employers to issue Contracts of Employment to all adult full- and part-time employees. It is prudent to ensure that each employee has signed the copy that remains in their personal file. It can do no harm, and may serve you well, if the unthinkable happens.

The Human Rights Act

Increasingly, this European Union drafted legislation is being cited in courts. Because it deals with general matters such as a 'right to privacy', it can affect virtually any aspect of employment, for example the use of video surveillance equipment. It applies to employees of organizations large and small, and makes it still more vital that all organizations define the standards expected of employees at work.

If you go expecting to lose

Experience shows that many SMEs do just that – and so they usually do. The penalties are becoming ever greater for organizations which take that approach; the maximum award of compensation for unfair dismissal in 2001 amounted to £50 000 (excluding costs) – sufficient to bankrupt many small businesses.

● For sex or race discrimination, the compensation that can be awarded is unlimited. Very large awards have already been made, as you will see from the examples given in Section 3, 'Where there's blame, there lies a claim'.

Larger organizations, too, often make it hard for themselves. Cases emerge where an employee has 'stacked up' five 'final written warnings' over a short period of time.

- How can that employee's employer expect the 'final, final' one to be taken seriously?

So, if instead of a sixth 'final written warning' the employee is dismissed, there is a good chance of an action for Unfair Dismissal succeeding.

- This would be especially true if other employees can be proved to have numerous warnings on file and are still employed. The lack of consistency alone would make the employer's case hard to sustain.

Who may come in on the appellant's side?

The CRE (Commission for Racial Equality) or the EOC (Equal Opportunities Commission) may take up actions on behalf of appellants whose cases they believe to have wider interest. The Citizens' Advice Bureau (CAB) may also take up cases on behalf of an employee.

- So far as is known, no such organization ever takes the employer's side.
- Rather, they place expert and – in the case of the CRE and EOC – effectively unlimited resources at the disposal of the appellant.

The scent of potentially large awards of compensation may also encourage law firms and specialist claim firms to take up cases on a 'no win, no fee' basis.

- These may be a severe threat to the SME that lacks professional personnel or human resources management and cannot really afford to retain a solicitor.

TRADE UNIONS

A trade union may also take up the case of a member whom it believes has been badly treated. In practice, union officials are very careful to check that their members have a good case before committing resources to their aid. They also tend to ensure that there are documented grievance and disciplinary procedures in use, based on an agreed balance between their members' personal rights and their obligations to their employers. Usually, local agreements will be based on national working agreements that have been thought through very carefully, verified by the best available specialists in the field and negotiated through line by line with employers' representatives.

- Such agreements are normally models of good practice and should be perceived as fair and reasonable by a tribunal.

Managers working in a unionized environment are best advised to work closely with local and regional officials to promote an atmosphere of mutual trust, helping to ensure that agreements are followed in the spirit as well as to the letter.

The risk management approach to employment tribunals

It is normal now for organizations to assess the risks of many aspects of their activities. Under Health and Safety laws, this is effectively a statutory requirement, but prudent organizations adopt the same principle of risk assessment and reduction in other fields. Many judge managers accordingly by the results they achieve. Insurance claims for damage arising from faulty products or services are often treated as avoidable business costs. Therefore, it makes sense to treat claims arising from proven wrongful dismissal in the same way.

- In a large organization, a manager is not doing their job properly if they land their employer frequently before employment tribunals. Their costs are a symptom of inefficient management just as surely as are high levels of 'scrap' or business lost through failure to meet quality or service standards.
- In a SME-size organization, one tribunal decision going against the owners may be catastrophic. It makes good sense in enterprises of every size to strike a balance between
  - the cost of implementing fair, sound, documented employment procedures and
  - the potential costs of losing a case before an employment tribunal. Given the unlimited costs of losing an action for, say, unfair dismissal on the grounds of Racial Discrimination, it is unlikely that the balance will ever come down on the side of taking a chance that the unthinkable may never happen.
- A glance at the background cases quoted in this resource should convince anyone who still harbours doubts as to the value of acting fairly – and being prepared to prove it.

'Where there's blame, there lies a claim'

This catchy piece of doggerel is worth bearing in mind in our increasingly compensation-conscious culture. Increasingly, people are willing to pursue claims for compensation concerning every aspect of life, anywhere and everywhere they believe that 'blame' may attach to a third party. Employment is no exception:

- In 1999/2000 there were 164 500 applications to employment tribunals – a 46 per cent increase on the previous year.
- If anything, the subsequent trend has been upwards.

CASE HISTORIES

In this chapter, following on from a look at the importance of case law, you will find examples of actual claims that have reached an employment tribunal, or have been settled out of court. The cases are selected to illustrate a variety of situations and decisions. Some recent cases are included where a decision has not been reached; you might find it useful to think through the summary of facts given, and decide how you believe the tribunal might determine the outcome.

- In some cases, fault – or 'blame' – has been attributed to an employer and often substantial compensation awarded.

For convenience, this section is divided into four sections, into which you can 'dip' at any time according to the situation you need to review. The categories are:

- Unfair Dismissal – maximum compensation award £50 000 in 2001
- Sex Discrimination – maximum compensation award unlimited, can easily exceed £100 000
- Race Discrimination – maximum compensation award unlimited, can easily exceed £100 000
- Employment Practices that can affect tribunal decisions in any of the categories above – favourably or unfavourably, so far as an employer is concerned.

THE IMPORTANCE OF CASE LAW

Case law is a very significant aspect of law in this country, because court decisions frequently set precedents which 'bind' their successors. This is very important where a general point of law is concerned. Courts are not allowed to make laws for themselves, but how they interpret the law can be of the utmost importance, as the following case illustrates.

The Midland Bank case

This was a case decided on by the Court of Appeal in the summer of 2000, involving the dismissal by the Midland Bank of an employee, and it makes the point well.

An internal investigation by the bank concluded that a bank official had misappropriated and used the debit cards of three customers. After a disciplinary hearing, the official was found guilty of gross misconduct and dismissed. The former employee applied to an employment tribunal (ET), which held that the bank had accepted their internal investigation's findings too readily and uncritically. The bank then took the case on to the Employment Appeals Tribunal (EAT). The EAT upheld the right of the original tribunal to substitute their own view for that of the company both

- as to the reason and
- the reasonableness of a decision.

In other words, the EAT said that an ET was within its rights to say what they would have done in the circumstances of a case and compare it with what the organization actually did.

- If the organization's decision differed from that of the tribunal, then the tribunal's decision would supersede the original one.

This would have set a very significant precedent, changing the ground rules on which the 'reasonableness of the decision' was judged and could have set a precedent that other tribunals would have followed. However, when the case reached the Court of Appeal, the decision of the EAT and the ET was reversed. The judge sitting ruled that such 'second guessing' was not within the jurisdiction of a tribunal. He ruled that it was a fundamental change that was for Parliament to make, not the courts.

- Until such a change is made an employer may decide a case on the 'balance of probabilities' and that the decision to dismiss was reasonable in the circumstances.
- They do not have to prove, as in a criminal court, that their decision was correct 'beyond all reasonable doubt', or guess how the tribunal might have decided in their place.

ACTUAL CASES

The following summarized cases illustrate a variety of circumstances, which you may find helpful to compare with your own situations. They include decisions by tribunals that had various outcomes.

Unfair dismissal

Awards against employers

- A tribunal ordered that a British Airways pilot should be reinstated to his former job after ruling that he had been dismissed unfairly. His offence was being 'rude and abusive' to a woman who claimed falsely that another passenger was carrying a bomb. Initially, the pilot had been demoted, involving a salary reduction of £50 000 a year. When he appealed through the company's disciplinary procedures, his seniority was reduced by ten years – reducing his earnings again – and, after his final appeal, he was dismissed.
- £50 000 was awarded to the manager of a gypsy site for stress following his dismissal from his position.
- A 17-stone rail worker won compensation for unfair dismissal. He was too large to work in a ticket booth that the employer said was designed to house two people and was dismissed as being incapable of doing his work.
- A single mother was awarded 'minimal' compensation for Unfair Dismissal after six weeks' service. She was dismissed for taking time off to collect her sick son from school.

Applications that failed

- A Japanese-owned company was held to be justified in dismissing a female employee who was 'too nice' when speaking to people on the telephone, wasting time and money.

Matters pending

- Ten employees dismissed by Royal & Sun Alliance for using e-mail to forward obscene material are demanding reinstatement. Some of the images were said to be pornographic and others racist in character.

Sex discrimination

Settled out of court

- £70 000 was accepted by a female city trader who was made redundant while on maternity leave from the Nomura Bank after six years' service. The bank allegedly failed to consult her in accordance with their own procedures. She claimed Unfair Dismissal and Sex Discrimination. She claimed that she had been insulted by male colleagues who sent pornographic e-mails, asked by one to wear 'short, tight skirts' and by another to 'strip and give me a massage'. The bank said it was happy to settle out of court for a fraction of the £350 000 that she had hoped to be awarded.

Awards against employers

- £500 000 was awarded to a female investment banker. Her boss accused her of having 'slept with clients' and described her as being 'hot totty'. The bank was found guilty of Sex Discrimination, the vast award reflected the employee's earning potential.
- £20 000 was awarded to a female employee after one day's work. She was forced to leave her job – a potentially highly-paid one as a commodity trader in London – because she was pregnant.

Applications that failed

- A former 'Page 3' model lost her claim for Constructive Dismissal. She applied for work on a training scheme to learn about information technology but claimed that she was sent to do heavy and dirty work on a farm instead. The tribunal dismissed her case because she was 'out of time' in submitting her evidence. She had claimed £375 000 in compensation for pain, suffering and loss of potential future earnings as a model.
- Frances Bissel, chief cookery writer for *The Times* newspaper, lost her claim for Unfair Dismissal. She was paid £650 a week on a freelance basis and was held not to be an employee of the newspaper.

Matters pending

- Julie Bower, backed by the EOC, is claiming Constructive Dismissal, unequal pay, breach of contract and sex discrimination against Schroeder Securities Limited. She claims that her refusal to take male clients to 'hostess bars' led to her being forced out of the company and reduced her annual bonus to £25 000, from the £125 000 earned by men who did take clients to such bars. She also claims that she was ousted from a job paying £120 000 per annum because she had cancer and had become pregnant. Reeth Sack, the woman head of European Sales for the bank at the time, denies that the firm discriminated against women.
- Tao Ball, a female computer consultant, is alleging Unfair Dismissal and Sex Discrimination. She says that her former employer in a £25 000 a year job sent her pornographic e-mails and spread unsavoury rumours about her as well as trebling her workload. Her employer admitted sending such e-mails to selected members of staff who he claimed enjoyed receiving them, and claims that she resigned. He said that she was 'moody'. The case continues.

Race discrimination

Awards against employers

- £350 000 in total was awarded to a Sikh policeman, against whom the Metropolitan Police Force were found guilty of Racial Discrimination.
- £25 000 was awarded to a black delivery man who was held to have been racially abused by his colleagues. The abuse included locking him in a goods trailer during overnight stops and punching him in the face. The applicant claimed that, as well as racial abuse, two former colleagues 'picked on him because of his pronounced stammer'.

A case that did not reach an employment tribunal

- A policemen with 12 years' unblemished service was reinstated by the police authority's appeals tribunal. He had originally been 'required to resign' after he was reported to have called a fellow Sikh officer a 'wog' (which he denied) and complained that the Asian officer had received preferential treatment over millennium rotas. More than 1000 people, including many from ethnic minorities, signed a petition asking for his reinstatement. His dismissal penalty was reduced to a fine of 13 days' wages.

Matters pending

- An Irish sales manager claims that he left his job because colleagues called him

'Paddy' and 'Leprechaun'. He claims Constructive Dismissal and Race Discrimination. His employers claim that, though they did not dismiss him, he frequently left work early, worked untidily and crashed a number of company vehicles.

- A Jewish trader claims Constructive Dismissal from his £125 000 a year job in London. After six years of accepting taunts about his race such as being called 'Jew boy' and 'Yiddo', he drew the line at being asked to dress up as Hitler. When he refused and subsequently complained, he was demoted. He then resigned and obtained a post with a rival organization. The employers state that such 'horseplay' was common and that other staff members were required to dress as pixies or fairies. He in turn had called Gentiles 'Yoks'. If the applicant succeeds, he could be awarded £50 000 for unfair dismissal, plus unlimited damages for Race Discrimination. The employers had offered to pay £50 000 to a Jewish charity of the appellant's choice, an offer which he refused.

Employment practices

Some practices risk being discriminatory by their very nature.

'Word of mouth' recruitment, where jobs are not formally advertised, but simply 'put about' to likely candidates, whether within the organization or outside it, would almost certainly constitute discrimination. By its very nature, it prevents many potential applicants from applying for a job which they have not been told exists.

- It is good practice to advertise jobs on your notice boards, or in other ways to make all staff aware of them, and also to advertise through Job Centres or local employment agencies. This should give anyone interested a chance to apply on an equal footing.

'Father to son' recruitment or promotion practices, as formerly followed in the London docks and elsewhere, are openly discriminatory. If there are any equivalent practices in your organization, beware! They are bound to fall foul of disability, sex and race discrimination legislation. So too would any 'mother to daughter' equivalents.

Custom and practice can take many forms, some of which may be unwittingly discriminatory. If, for example, a group of managers meets at the golf club or other social venue such as the local pub and discusses business there, this may exclude people who for various reasons cannot be there. If business decisions about personnel, policy, promotion issues and the like are discussed and made there, there is a substantial risk of offending the spirit of the legislation – and possibly its letter too.

- It is far better to make business decisions on business premises, during business hours and to ensure that you obtain the input of everyone who would normally expect to be involved.

The situation described may not match your own. But any 'informal' management structure that ignores the formal one under which employees are told that they work is likely to exclude them from matters with which they have a right to be involved and may be discriminatory.

Staff appraisal systems

Staff appraisal systems, often linked to objectives and targets for the coming period, are used in many organizations. On the face of things, they are an excellent, professional means of managing objectively and giving employees the chance to give, as well as receive, feedback. However, they can be sources of discontent if employees believe that they are not operated consistently, as between employees in the same department or between different departments. If records of appraisal can be shown to suggest that

● some employees are passed over for promotion without good cause despite more favourable appraisal results than those who are promoted,
● or that merit awards do not follow appraisal results consistently, then this may well be evidence of discrimination against a particular employee.

Normally, every employee should read and sign his or her appraisal, indicating any issues raised with the appraiser. Gratuitous comments added after the employee has done so will not help an employer's case before a tribunal, especially if they read like some of these, all taken from real appraisals:

'Since my last report, this employee has reached rock bottom and continued to dig.'

'Works well under supervision when cornered like a rat in a trap.'

'He sets low personal standards and consistently fails to meet them.'

'This employee is depriving a village somewhere of an idiot.'

'This girl has delusions of adequacy.'

'She's so dense, light bends round her.'

'This employee should go far – the sooner he starts, the better.'

The author of the last comment would probably wish that he or she was a very long way from an employment tribunal if that literary effort should ever be produced to it by an employee alleging discrimination.

● You don't need to be a model of political correctness to see that these remarks are generally subjective, offensive and imply that the object of them is likely to be treated less favourably than other employees.
● Appraisal systems should concentrate on matters that can be assessed objectively and debated rationally.

Records of disciplinary warnings

It is good practice to keep a record of all disciplinary actions on an employee's file, including improvement periods and the date on which they expired. But, beware the situation of an employee who has five 'final written warnings' on file. Subject to reasonable improvement periods and just investigatory procedures, a 'final written warning' should mean just what it says. If the employee transgresses again in a serious manner, especially if the offence is related to the existing warning, then dismissal should be the next and final stage. 'Ducking the issue' will usually create more problems than it solves: how could you possibly expect anyone with even two 'final' written warnings to take the next one seriously, or expect to be dismissed?

Personal Attitude Questionnaire

Use this questionnaire to rate your attitude towards fairness in matters concerning employing people. When you have completed and scored the questionnaire, check your rating using the explanatory grid that follows. A blank copy of the questionnaire is provided as one of the Appendices to this Resource. The best way to use it is to photocopy the master and use it:

- firstly, before you undertake any of the other activities in this programme
- secondly, when you have completed all the activities from the programme that you intend to use.

This will give you an idea by how much, if at all, your approach to disciplinary matters and employment tribunals has altered.

Rate yourself against each question from 1 to 5:
1 strongly disagree
2 tend to disagree
3 open to persuasion
4 tend to agree
5 strongly agree.

 REPRODUCED FROM *HOW TO AVOID EMPLOYMENT TRIBUNALS*, COLIN EVERSON, GOWER, ALDERSHOT

Question Number	Personal attitude questionnaire statement	Your rating				
		1	2	3	4	5
1	I believe it is a manager's right to manage and the law shouldn't interfere with how I manage people.					
2	Employees have had a hard time from employers for too long now – it's time something was done to tilt the balance in their favour.					
3	Paperwork systems are a waste of time – managers have better things to do with their time.					
4	Employment tribunals don't affect smaller organizations.					
5	We can run our organization on the basis of mutual trust – we don't need loads of systems to help us get on together.					
6	Once the management has decided to get rid of someone, there's nothing an employee or the law can do about it, providing you've got watertight systems in place.					
7	The law doesn't expect smaller organizations to keep records like the bigger ones do – they haven't the time or the need.					
8	Employees caught stealing should be sacked immediately – it doesn't matter if they've been there 20 minutes or 20 years.					
9	Induction training is essential to let people know where they stand from day one.					
10	Doing everything 'by the book' means you can get rid of anyone you need to, without any comeback – that's what the systems are for.					
11	Briefing sessions for employees are just an excuse for them to stop working and gripe about their jobs. I'll soon tell them if they don't come up to scratch.					
12	You should make allowance for employees' individual circumstances when deciding on disciplinary action.					
	YOUR TOTALS					

REPRODUCED FROM *HOW TO AVOID EMPLOYMENT TRIBUNALS*, COLIN EVERSON, GOWER, ALDERSHOT

Your rating

Score	Possible interpretation
12–20	There could be some inconsistencies in the way you have responded – please check your answers. If you still come up with the same score, you may be at cross purposes with yourself as to what are your real beliefs as a manager.
21–32	You are probably by preference a 'dove', who believes in fairness, tolerance and understanding. This is especially true at the lower end of this band, so you may need to take care that others do not try to take advantage of your approach.
33–39	Implies that you are very open to persuasion, especially if you scored twelve 3s to achieve a total of 36!
40–50	This band suggests that you are a 'hawk' by instinct, perhaps because of unfortunate experience. If you come out towards the top end of the band, you need to take care that your approach does not lead you into unnecessary conflicts and unwinnable situations at tribunals!
51–60	There could be some inconsistencies in the way you have answered – please check your answers. If you still come up with the same score, you may be at cross purposes with yourself as to what are your real beliefs as a manager.

Case study 1

AN APPLICATION ALLEGING UNFAIR DISMISSAL

George Kempton and the Citizens' Advice Bureau vs. *Speedwell Pies and Pasties*

INTRODUCTION

This case study is the longest of the three and in many ways the most complex. It is modelled very closely on a real case and all the events and the sequence of events are very close to what actually happened. Read it carefully and use the discussion break-points provided to review your own thoughts and opinions of the way in which it progressed and was conducted.

An application alleging Unfair Dismissal

George Kempton and the Citizens' Advice Bureau vs. *Speedwell Pies and Pasties*

PROCEDURAL CHECKLIST

A checklist is provided as part of this Resource on page 61. It has been annotated to show how Speedwell's procedures stand up to detailed scrutiny. A blank copy is provided in Appendix 2 on page 93, which you can use as a check on your own procedures.

TRIBUNAL PROCEDURES

When you have read through the case, you may find it helpful to look at Tribunal Procedures on page 70, where there are charts showing the logic that is used to determine whether there has been Unfair Dismissal.

A BAD MONDAY MORNING FOR PETER LEWES

Peter Lewes arrived at Speedwell on a dreary Monday morning, and said 'Good Morning' briefly to everyone as he checked over the site before dealing with the day's post. He opened it in his office on the first floor. Amongst the usual welter of circulars, trade publications, appeals from charities and catalogues from their stationery supplier announcing 'still more unbelievable deals' was an official-looking envelope. Inside it was a summons for him to appear before an Employment Tribunal in a few weeks' time in a town about fifty miles from the site.

George Kempton, an employee who had been dismissed several weeks previously, was claiming that he had been 'unfairly dismissed'. Though Peter was not exactly surprised, he had begun to believe that the incident on a Saturday morning had receded into the past and that his former employee had perhaps accepted the justice of his fate. Instead of which, Peter was now faced with all the distracting hassle of a tribunal hearing, a potential maximum award of £50 000 to a man who had already caused him much trouble – and possible legal fees, which Peter could not afford, on top of any award made should he lose.

Summary dismissal was a severe penalty and he had not imposed it without much soul-searching. Now, he felt a knot in his stomach and asked himself yet again whether he had acted fairly – and whether he would be able to prove to a tribunal that he had done so. Wearily, he sat down to consider, go over the case once again in his mind and decide what to do. He began by reviewing the people directly involved, starting with himself.

The Management

Peter Lewes (aged 47) – proprietor for the past 11 months of a food manufacturing, wholesaling and retailing organization employing around 16 full time equivalent (FTE) staff, 24 full-time and part-time employees in all. He was working at home on the Saturday in question but in telephone contact with the organization via Jackie York, Deputy Manageress.

Jennifer Lewes (aged 39) – wife of Peter; not involved in the organization on a day-to-day basis, deals with marketing issues and financial accounts.

Rose Stockbridge (aged 24) – Manageress of the retail part of the organization. With eight years service, beginning as a 'Saturday girl', she was promoted about a year ago, just before the present proprietors bought the organization. Not working on the Saturday in question.

Jackie York (aged 36) – Deputy Manageress of the retail organization. Works part time, including most Saturdays. Fourteen years service, broken by a period of two years. Deputizing for Rose on the Saturday in question.

The Staff

Only those both working and affected by the incidents are listed.

Retail

Emma Gatwick (aged 16) – Saturday Girl, three months service, engaged by Rose Stockbridge.

Production

Anne Chester – full-time general production and hygiene assistant, six months service, engaged by Peter.

George Kempton (aged 38) – a long-serving full-time production employee, 23 years service. Joined the organization on leaving school.

Martin Taunton (aged 34) – full-time production assistant, two years service. Formerly worked for a much larger organization in a similar field.

Shaun Derby (aged 36) – full-time production assistant, 10 months service, engaged by present proprietor when he moved to the area.

 REPRODUCED FROM *HOW TO AVOID EMPLOYMENT TRIBUNALS*, COLIN EVERSON, GOWER, ALDERSHOT

John Phoenix (aged 57 years) – delivery driver, 18 months service. Works mainly from about 4 a.m. to 9.30 or 10 a.m. Collects money from some 'cash' wholesale customers on Saturday morning and so tends to be rather later returning to base.

The Customers

Only those present during the incident are mentioned.

Mrs Exeter – a long-standing 'regular', who always comes in on a Saturday morning.

'Lady' Fieldstreet – another Saturday morning customer.

The Background

Peter and Jennifer bought the Speedwell organization from the previous owners, who had run it for about three years (making and selling, to both retail and wholesale customers, a range of pies, pasties and a limited range of flour confectionery items). The Leweses, who have other business interests, took on the existing staff at the time. The intention was to run Speedwell through the existing Production Manager (David Brighton) and Rose, the Shop Manageress. Both had been appointed by the previous owners. Peter spent about three days a week at the site (about forty miles from home until they could move closer) plus alternate Saturdays; Jennifer spent much less time there. Peter made a point of being present on occasions during the night, when most production tasks were in progress.

Over eleven months, the Leweses introduced many changes and improvements to working arrangements, including those involving health, safety and hygiene. All of these had been given scant attention by the previous owners! Among these changes were an arrangement with a local laundry to supply and launder sets of overalls (allowing two sets of clean overalls per production employee per week). Production staff were also issued with a pair of safety shoes, on the strict understanding that they must be worn at work – and only at work. These would be replaced annually. Peter also installed a shower, at a cost of several hundred pounds, for use by production staff, which they were allowed to use as often as they wished to. He installed a proper rest room and changing room for female employees, who had previously used a corner of a store room as an unofficial rest area.

On the sales front, Peter negotiated a contract with the local hospital to supply a range of items to their visitors' coffee shops. Obtaining this contract involved undergoing a stringent independent Hygiene Audit, at a cost of several hundred pounds, and accepting a number of conditions about the premises and the behaviour of staff. All production staff were informed about – and involved fully in – the changes required to secure the new – and vital – business.

The chief events leading to the eventual employment tribunal hearing triggered by George Kempton were as follows:

- Retail sales were badly affected by a large roadworks scheme in the immediate area, which made the market square a mess and took away many parking spaces.

- The Production Manager's role became redundant and Peter helped him find acceptable alternative employment in a similar organization.
- Peter then negotiated a deal with the production staff whereby they became effectively an autonomous working group, or 'cell', subject to his general direction. All production staff were granted a 12½ per cent pay rise to recognize the increased responsibility they now accepted, for example daily production scheduling and ingredients stock control.
- Peter instigated a programme of regular briefing for all staff, including Saturday staff, to keep them informed about the changes he was making. Briefing sessions, backed up by notes on the new notice boards, placed emphasis on health, safety and hygiene matters – especially concerning the hospital's requirements.
- The improvements which Peter made, coupled with developing a close working relationship with the local Environmental Health Officers led to the award of the local authority's gold award for food hygiene standards.
- After Brighton's departure, it became clear that there had been tensions between him and both the production and retail staff. On at least two occasions, this had led to physical confrontation between Brighton, Kempton and Taunton. No reports were made of this at the time to Peter, nor were previous incidents mentioned by the former owners.
- Peter introduced formal Contracts of Employment, which specified detailed Terms and Conditions of Employment. He used the format recommended by the Trade Association. The Contracts were discussed fully and individually with every staff member, before they signed what to most of them was a highly unfamiliar document.
- The Terms and Conditions specified clearly what would constitute 'Gross Industrial Misconduct' for which the penalty would be summary dismissal. The implications of this penalty were made clear to all staff members. There was no union involvement at the site. Peter would have been perfectly happy had there been, having worked mostly in larger organizations and appreciating the positive role which Unions frequently play. Not surprisingly, no member of staff had any formal written warnings on file, or any recorded verbal warnings.
- For production staff, the contracts included reference to the new 'semi-autonomous' working arrangements and their responsibilities under them.
- All regular staff who did not already hold the Basic Food Hygiene Certificate were enrolled on a course run by the local hospital. All the male production staff already held this award, or an equivalent qualification from previous training.

POINT FOR DISCUSSION BREAK

Assess the background work that Peter had done concerning employment systems, particularly concerning

● communications with staff
● changes to working arrangements in production
● welfare arrangements (for example laundry provision)
● issue of Contracts of Employment and Terms and Conditions of Employment.

Do you think that Peter's actions were

● fair?
● consistent as between the employees?

In general terms, where would you rate him on the Personal Questionnaire you have completed for yourself? From the evidence you have, does he appear to be a hawk or a dove by inclination?

The First Incident

About four weeks before the incident that resulted in George Kempton's summary dismissal, Peter arrived at the site at 8.30 a.m. and was approached immediately by Anne Chester. She told him there had been an incident involving herself, George Kempton and a wholesale customer, Sue Hurst, who had come in to complain about human hair found inside a pie. The customer had spoken initially to Rose Stockbridge, who summoned George to talk to her as he was the longest-serving member of the production team. According to Anne, his overalls were dirty, he was not wearing a hat and wore filthy trainers rather than the safety shoes with which he had been issued. The customer told him that he 'smelled'. She also commented on a bicycle which was propped against a table in the production area. Anne confirmed it had been there and, under questioning by Peter, said it belonged to George Kempton.

George Kempton retorted that the hair was nothing to do with him and told the customer that probably it was one of hers. Anne had to intervene to calm things down. This all happened on a 'light' production day (Thursday). George had gone home before Peter arrived and left no message about the incident. Fortunately, no retail customers became involved. The offending hair appeared to match George Kempton's colouring but, short of conducting forensic tests, there was no way of proving it was one of his. Peter had no doubt that it had been baked into the product.

Peter dealt first with the angry customer, involving him in a visit to her premises. Sue Hurst's account, broadly speaking, agreed with that of Anne. She said it was not the first time that she had seen George Kempton in a less than hygienic state and that one more such incident would cause her to take her business elsewhere. Peter then rang George at home and told him that he would investigate the incident at 9.30 the following morning.

This he did, in the presence of Rose Stockbridge. George Kempton was very quiet and at first refused to answer Peter's questions. After hearing the accounts of Anne Chester and Sue Hurst, however:

- he eventually admitted that the bicycle was his and said he feared it would be stolen if he left it outside. Other members of staff who cycled to work simply chained their machines to a nearby railing.
- he said he was not wearing dirty overalls (this morning, he was immaculate, even at the end of his work) and flatly denied the other comments made by Sue.
- he denied being rude to a customer but, when further pressed, claimed that 'She only got what she asked for'.

Peter asked George to withdraw, while he considered what action he would take. He talked it through with Rose before coming to a conclusion. She had not been directly involved in the incident, but had gained a general impression of it and had known George throughout her eight years working at Speedwell. She said that it looked very bad for him but interceded on his behalf, saying that he was 'not a bad sort' normally and usually produced very good quality products.

POINT FOR DISCUSSION BREAK

What would you have done? Would you, for example, have

- done nothing, perhaps on the basis that only 'hearsay' evidence was available?
- issued an Informal Warning or 'admonishment'?
- issued a Recorded Verbal Warning?
- issued a First Written Warning as specified in George's Terms and Conditions of Employment?
- issued a Second and Final Written Warning, again as specified in George's terms and conditions of employment?
- dismissed him with the notice due under his Contract? If so, could you
  - have required him to work his notice? or
  - bought out the notice?
- dismissed him summarily for Gross Industrial Misconduct?
- imposed some other penalty (e.g. suspension with or without pay for a set period)?

What Peter Actually Did

Peter recalled George Kempton into his office and told him that his conduct constituted Gross Industrial Misconduct, for which he could have been summarily dismissed. However:

- He had long service.
- There were no records of former disciplinary offences on George's file.
- He (Peter) had not witnessed the event personally or had any direct previous experience of misconduct by him.
- The customer had accepted Peter's apology on George's behalf.
- Rose had spoken up for George and she had known him for several years.

Peter told George Kempton that he had therefore decided not to dismiss him. Instead, he issued a Final Written Warning, which would remain in force during an 'improvement period' of six months. Any further offences of a similar nature within that period would lead to summary dismissal. He would issue the written warning formally the next day, together with a record of the disciplinary hearing, both of which would be retained in George's personal file.

Both these things he duly did. George appeared to accept the warning with a reasonable grace and actually thanked Peter for 'giving him another chance'. He said the notes of the hearing seemed accurate and that he had nothing to add. He signed the copy that Peter retained on his file. Peter hoped that this would be an end to the matter – but in this he was to be disappointed.

The Second Incident

The facts, as they emerged to Peter on a Saturday morning about four weeks later, were as follows.

As usual Peter rang the Speedwell site at around 8 a.m., to check that there were no problems requiring his intervention. He spoke to Jackie, who confirmed that things were OK, apart from some problems with production, and as George was 'sorting them out now' Peter did not need to be involved.

He next spoke to Jackie at about 11.30 a.m. She appeared rather distracted, but was unwilling to say why. When he pressed her, she admitted that there had been another incident involving George Kempton. He had already gone home, but Jackie said that several other people had been involved, including two customers, who had overheard a part of it, and Anne Chester, who had also gone home – in a distressed state.

Peter later had an angry phone call from Anne's husband, who would not allow him to speak directly to her. She was threatening not to return to work. Eventually, Peter persuaded her husband that she should come in on the following Monday morning, to tell him in her own words what had happened. Peter also rang George, but there was no reply – he had probably gone fishing, his main interest away from work. Peter decided that he must investigate the incident fully on Monday morning, when most of the people involved would be at work. It would be tiresome, but it was essential.

Monday Morning

Before talking to anyone else, Peter found George in the bakery, took him into the production office and explained that he would be holding a disciplinary hearing that morning, once he had talked to the various people involved. George was noticeably clean-shaven and tidy this morning and was wearing the safety shoes issued.

What the witnesses said

Jackie York said:

> 'I didn't want to bother you at first about the mess-up in production. It was worse than I thought though – a whole batch had almost gone up in smoke. It was

completely unsaleable and had to be remade – this left us short of stock for a couple of hours. I spoke to George and Martin about it – Martin told me on the quiet that George had simply forgotten to check the oven and seemed in a very bad temper generally. He didn't know why – he was just trying to keep out of his way. It all seemed to die down for a bit, just until the time that John Phoenix came back in at about eleven o'clock. I was just talking to him about the hospital delivery – they'd gone a bit short because of the spoiled products – when all hell broke loose. You know those heavy metal tables in the production area?' Peter nodded. 'Well, it sounded as though someone was throwing them about – made a noise like cymbals clashing. Then, I heard voices shouting – they got louder and I reckoned it was Anne and George. Then, they appeared, shouting at each other – I couldn't understand what they were saying, but it certainly wasn't a friendly chat they were having!'

'Did anyone else hear all this?' Peter asked.

'Well, John of course. And there were two regular customers in the shop – Mrs Exeter for one. And the one we call 'Lady' Fieldstreet 'cause that's where she lives, we can't understand what she calls herself and she expects us to grovel! Emma, the Saturday girl was there and she must have heard too. Sharon was on a break upstairs, so I doubt she heard much.'

'And you couldn't work out at all what it was all about?' asked Peter.

'Well, it started in the production area, and so I didn't hear any of that – it seemed as if Anne was trying to get away from George when I saw her and all I heard were bits about cups of tea and bikes in the bakery and burnt pies. It didn't make much sense to me.'

Further questioning yielded little further information, other than that the two customers seemed shocked by the events they witnessed and that Jackie had done her best to smooth things over as the protagonists left the retail area, with John acting as a sort of 'chaperone'. It was to him that Peter turned next. Emma was back at school and Sharon did not normally work again until Wednesday. In any case, she had probably heard little or nothing of the incident.

John Phoenix pretty well confirmed what Jackie had said. He only added that, once he had gone with them back into the production area, they separated into their respective changing areas. He saw both leaving the premises a few minutes later. Martin and Shaun were annoyed that George had 'dropped them in it' leaving them to clear up the mess caused by the mistakes he had made. At this point, Anne Chester arrived. Peter asked her to tell him exactly what had happened, to the best of her recollection.

'Well,' she said, 'George was in a funny mood all morning. He's always resented you taking me on anyway and he's told me more than once women have no place in here – they should stick to the shop. Anyway, I think he sees me as a "spy" for you – especially over hygiene – which you know I'm not. It all came to a head when Shaun or Martin – I forget which – noticed the smell of burning and rushed over to the oven. They tried to pull George's leg about it at first – but he wasn't in the mood for joking. He flew into a rage right off, called them some unrepeatable names and told them they should have kept their wits about them. Then he

 REPRODUCED FROM *HOW TO AVOID EMPLOYMENT TRIBUNALS*, COLIN EVERSON, GOWER, ALDERSHOT

noticed me by the sink and said to me, "Why don't you do something useful for a change and make some tea – it's all you're good for anyway. If you were any use, you'd have noticed those pies burning." Well, I wasn't having that and I told him so in no uncertain terms. I told him I don't work for him – and I told him he should get his bike out of the place too – the filthy thing was leaning against a table again. If I can chain mine up outside, why can't he? He threw the bike down on the ground and then started shaking one of the big stainless steel tables – made a terrible din. I thought he was trying to tip it over me, so I thought it best to get out into the shop. I was pretty angry myself by now, I admit it, but he started on me for no reason at all. He still wouldn't leave me alone, followed me until we came across John and Jackie in the stock area, by the phone. Seeing them and a couple of customers in the shop calmed him down a bit and John was quite helpful too. Soon after, I went home – and I'm not sure I want to work here any more.'

That was pretty well all Anne had to say, and so Peter went on with the painstaking process by talking to Martin and Shaun individually. They were reluctant to talk at first, not wishing as Martin put it, 'to shop a mate.' However, when Peter summarized the stories told him by Jackie, John and Anne, they both became more forthcoming. They confirmed all the basic facts as Peter had already gathered them, and added some extra points themselves:

- George had been in a vile temper that morning and was once again in a dirty state.
- There had been another flare up the previous day, again with George picking on Anne and saying there was no place for her in a 'man's world'.
- His bike was there again despite their telling him that if Peter found it there again, there would be 'hell to pay', especially with the hospital contract being so important to him.
- The burnt products were really George's fault – he just forgot about them though he was minding the oven at the time. They'd tried to make light of it and help him out, but he wouldn't listen. Then, he started the row with Anne, really for no reason at all – she'd already made a pot of tea earlier that day and they usually took turns.

Finally, Martin, whom Peter normally found a reasonable individual, added a couple of observations in confidential tones.

'We've been wondering what to do for a couple of weeks now. It's not only his bad temper – and we've covered up some mistakes for him before – but, well, some nights he really turns up dirty and smelly. Those rotten old shoes he wears sometimes. And he doesn't shave always, says he can't shave in works time but that's when it grows. Well, it's not very nice for us – and if the hospital blokes or an EHO did an unannounced visit, well, all our jobs could be at risk. He's the longest serving – so he'd probably be the last to go if you had to cut back – at least, that's what they always did at National Bakeries. The union had a "last in, first out" agreement.'

Peter told all the interviewees that he would ask them to sign statements that he would write up from his notes and his recollection of the interviews. They agreed quite readily to this.

Peter now asked Rose Stockbridge to join him as an independent witness to the disciplinary hearing he would conduct with George Kempton. As Rose had not been present on Saturday or when he talked to the witnesses, he felt that she was a reasonable person to sit with him. She had also been helpful to George's cause following the previous incident.

He asked George to join them and asked for his account of Saturday morning. Rose, as asked, did not intervene other than to ask him to repeat or clarify occasional points. At first, he was taciturn and said virtually nothing. When Peter mentioned the accounts of the witnesses, he did not either agree with them, or challenge them. He admitted bringing the bicycle into a food area, despite the previous warning; denied that his clothes or his person were unhygienic and blamed Anne categorically for the mistake over the oven. He repeated that women had no place in a bakery – they were too slow and not strong enough to do their fair share of the work. He denied throwing the bicycle at Anne, or 'throwing the tables about'. Finally, when pressed again about poor personal hygiene in a food production area, he said, 'I don't have time to shave or have a bath before I come here – you make me start too early.' Asked if he had ever used the new shower, he said, 'Once or twice at the end of a shift.' Peter then asked him to withdraw whilst he considered his decision.

POINT FOR DISCUSSION BREAK

Do you believe that Peter conducted a fair investigation into the second incident involving George Kempton? Do you think he could have done anything differently, to ensure that George had a proper chance to put his side of the case? What action would you now take concerning George? Would you, for example

- do nothing, on the basis that only 'hearsay' evidence was available?
- issue a second final written warning?
- demote him to another job?
- dismiss him with the notice due under his contract? If so, would you
  - have required him to work his notice? or
  - bought out the notice?
- dismiss him summarily for Gross Industrial Misconduct?
- impose some other penalty (e.g. suspension with or without pay for a set period)?

If you choose dismissal, with or without notice, do you believe the evidence, as collected by Peter, would be sufficient to prove to an Employment Tribunal that his dismissal was 'fair'?   YES/NO

Peter's Verdict

After a brief discussion with Rose, really to confirm that she agreed with his notes about various points, Peter told her that he had decided to dismiss George Kempton summarily for Gross Industrial Misconduct. He asked George to return to his office and, still in Rose's presence, briefly announced his decision to him and explained why he had come to it, as follows:

- George was only a few weeks into a Final Written Warning that still had several months to run.
- A number of the present offences, attested to by several witnesses, were directly related to that final warning.
- Some of those that were not related would in themselves constitute Gross Misconduct. Verbal abuse of a colleague, threatening behaviour and abusing company property certainly would. If he had a genuine grievance against Anne Chester, he could have followed the Grievance Procedure in his Terms and Conditions of Employment.
- Once again, customers had witnessed his behaviour.
- As a responsible manufacturer of food, Peter could not permit an employee to flout standards of hygiene. The law and his commercial reputation required him to protect consumers' health.
- Other offences were serious too, in particular the loss of production and behaviour towards his male colleagues.

He then asked George Kempton if he had anything further to say and reminded him of his right of appeal under the Speedwell's disciplinary procedure. Kempton said something indistinct about 'being determined to get him' but added nothing else. Nor did he apologize for his conduct, or complain of any specific grievances against Anne. He left the office to collect his things and departed shortly afterwards. Meantime, Rose said to Peter, 'I know he's been a fool and he brought most of this on himself. But he's worked here a long time – couldn't you give him one more chance?'.

The Appeal

A few days later, a brief letter arrived signed by Mrs Kempton, announcing George's wish to exercise his right of appeal. A date was set for the following Tuesday, at 11 a.m. As set out in the procedure, Jennifer Lewes would hear his appeal, as she was not involved in the day-to-day running of the organization and had no direct involvement in the disciplinary hearing. In the meantime, Peter had posted a 'written statement of reasons for dismissal' to George Kempton, setting out the matters that had been explained to him after the hearing.

George arrived, smartly dressed and accompanied by his wife and another person, who was apparently someone with whom she worked. Peter refused to allow the third person to attend the appeal, as having no interest in the matter. None of his former colleagues was willing to appear with him, although this would have been allowed by the appeal procedure. With a less than good grace, Mr and Mrs Kempton accepted Peter's ruling and Jennifer Lewes conducted the appeal. Rose again provided an independent witness to the proceedings.

Mrs Kempton did almost all the talking, George saying virtually nothing throughout the twenty minutes or so that it lasted. She did not question the facts of the incidents, but concentrated chiefly upon the unfairness, as she saw it, of sacking a long-serving employee who carried the organization on his shoulders. She demanded that he be reinstated forthwith and his earnings be made up. No one had complained about his conduct before they took over the organization, she said. It had all started when Anne Chester was taken on. Jennifer listened to her points, asked a few questions to clarify the grounds on which they were appealing, summed up what they had said and concluded by saying that she would consider their appeal and let them know her decision in writing, as required by the agreed procedure.

When they had gone, Rose once more said that she wished George could be given a 'second chance' and that she admired the way Mrs Kempton had stood up for her husband – she would have done the same. Jennifer said she would take some time to consider her verdict.

POINT FOR DISCUSSION BREAK

What verdict might you have reached in the circumstances?

- Was Jennifer Lewes the right person to hear the appeal? If not, who would you suggest might have heard it?
- Was it reasonable for Peter to exclude the third person from the hearing? If not, what purpose might he have served?
- Do you believe that the appeal was conducted fairly?
- What verdict would you have reached bearing in mind
  - the facts of the case which led to George's summary dismissal
  - the witness statements
  - the appeal which Mrs Kempton presented to Jennifer Lewes
  - any other matters you believe relevant?

The Appeal Verdict

Jennifer decided that there were no grounds to overturn the original decision. This she decided because

- no new factual evidence had been presented
- the established facts were not disputed
- no valid mitigating circumstances were introduced
- the fairness of the disciplinary procedure itself was not questioned
- much – if not all – of what Mrs Kempton said was irrelevant to the case. She was simply stating that she believed George had been treated unfairly, but without bringing any evidence to show how this was so
- the fact that none of George Kempton's production colleagues would 'speak for him' – and indeed had all signed statements to confirm the conduct he had been dismissed for – was much more telling evidence.

Jennifer wrote briefly to George Kempton, confirming that his appeal had failed, with a brief summary of the first four points given above. Nothing further was heard until the letter arrived from the Employment Tribunal on that Monday morning.

ACAS Become Involved

A few days after the Employment Tribunal notice arrived, Peter received a phone call from Derek Hamilton, at ACAS, the Advisory, Conciliation and Arbitration Service. Hamilton said the George Kempton case had been referred to him and he would like to meet Peter and review it before it came to tribunal. Peter, who had dealt with ACAS

 REPRODUCED FROM *HOW TO AVOID EMPLOYMENT TRIBUNALS*, COLIN EVERSON, GOWER, ALDERSHOT

previously and found them helpful, agreed to do so. Mr Hamilton spoke frankly about George Kempton's case.

'He'll be represented by the CAB (Citizens' Advice Bureau). He won't have a solicitor at the hearing, one of the local CAB staff will represent him. If it goes to tribunal, will you have a solicitor on your side?'

'I doubt it,' said Peter, 'I believe our case is very strong and it will add an unnecessary expense.'

Hamilton nodded. 'I agree,' he said. 'The CAB have told him that he has a very weak case, based on the facts as he presents them and the various documents they've seen. They've shown them all to me and I agree that he is in a very weak position. The CAB advisor also thinks he wouldn't come over very well in court..'

'In that case,' interjected Peter, 'surely it's in everyone's interests for him to call the whole thing off now.'

'. . . nevertheless, he is determined to go ahead,' resumed Hamilton. 'Looking at it from his point of view, he could stand to gain £50 000.' He looked pointedly at Peter. 'At your expense. He can't lose anything – if it goes to tribunal, the CAB will represent him for nothing, he'll be able to claim expenses for the journeys – all he needs to do is write one letter saying you dismissed him unfairly.'

'But surely, in view of the CAB's opinion, which you agree with – he hasn't a chance of winning. The whole hearing will be a waste of everyone's time.'

'That may be true, but it's not really relevant so far as he is concerned. He simply says you dismissed him unfairly and that he is entitled to compensation from you – at least, that's what will be said on his behalf. The odds may be 100 to 1 against him, but £50 000 is still worth trying for. You must try to see it from his point of view – working here all those years, no recorded problems until you come along, then in less than a year, he's out of a job. No notice, no severance pay of any kind, no written reference of the kind that would help him get another job.'

Peter said, 'In fact, I believe that he does have another job, so he isn't even out of work. His new employer rang me for a verbal reference. It's a big vegetable packing set-up. I said nothing to injure his chances – he won't be in direct contact with high-risk food and will be under much closer supervision than here, so I could honestly tell them that I saw no reason not to employ him.'

'Nevertheless, that doesn't alter his case,' said Hamilton, 'the tribunal doesn't have to award the maximum amount, but they might make an award somewhere between nothing and the top limit – say £10 000 or £15 000.' He looked quizzically at Peter. 'Could you afford to pay that amount?'

'Certainly not,' retorted Peter. 'We're struggling to keep the business going at the moment. Even £5000 would be a disaster. But, our case is so strong – as both you and the CAB accept – that surely there is no risk of him winning. We've got signed statements from all the witnesses, including his own colleagues, which all confirm what happened. I've also spoken to Kevin Perth – he runs the hospital catering set-up. Kevin had heard what happened on his bush telegraph. Once I explained to him what I'd done and why, he said he would be prepared to act as a witness on our behalf. The violence and the lost production weren't really his concern – but the hygiene standards definitely were. He would state categorically on oath that Kempton's abysmal hygiene standards could have cost us their business – worth around £30 000 in annual sales, probably £20 000 in gross profit. That would have put us out of business, almost certainly.'

'All that you say is no doubt true,' Hamilton concurred. 'And yet, there is still a chance that, despite it all, the Tribunal may accept his claim that he was dismissed unfairly. If they do, there's no effective appeal for you.'

'So what do you suggest I do?' Peter asked. 'As I understand it, ACAS is neutral in these matters – so you should be able to offer me independent advice.'

'Well,' said Hamilton, 'my opinion is that the risk to you is sufficient for you to consider making an offer to him, stop the affair coming to a tribunal at all. I'm sure the CAB can convince him that he may lose if he proceeds, so half a loaf is better than nothing. A bird in the hand . . .'

'. . . But in this case, I shall be giving him the bird – and feeding it for a long time too!' Peter interrupted with some heat.

They continued discussing the advantages and disadvantages of Hamilton's advice for some minutes. Eventually, Hamilton left without hearing a firm decision from Peter, who undertook to think it over and call him in a couple of days, having discussed the matter with Jennifer.

POINT FOR DISCUSSION BREAK

What would you have done in Peter's situation? You might carry out a risk assessment on the basis of the facts as presented. Remember that the maximum award against Peter is a 'one time' £50 000 and that losing the hospital's business would cost around £20 000 in lost profits annually on a continuing basis. When you have weighed up the risks, you might choose between the following options:

- Agree to negotiate an out of court settlement setting a maximum that you are prepared to pay. If so, what would it be bearing in mind Speedwell's financial difficulties and the threat of a maximum £50 000 award by the Tribunal?
- Let Kempton proceed to the Tribunal, believing your case to be too strong to fail. If so, would you engage a solicitor to act on your behalf, and how much would you be prepared to pay for legal advice?

What Peter and Jennifer Decided

In fact, Peter and Jennifer decided not to offer an out of court 'option' to Kempton. They reasoned that, should they do so

- He would 'scent' money and almost certainly look for an increased offer from them, however much they 'put on the table' initially
- If the case then went to tribunal, the fact of their having made an offer would weaken their case, suggesting they had doubts about the fairness of their actions.

 REPRODUCED FROM *HOW TO AVOID EMPLOYMENT TRIBUNALS*, COLIN EVERSON, GOWER, ALDERSHOT

Their decision was taken largely 'on principle'. They believed their case was very strong – and that should they waver, they would set a precedent that could influence the behaviour of other staff members for the worse.

They also decided not to use a solicitor, but rather to ask an experienced personnel manager whom they both knew well to speak on their behalf as a 'friend'.

Preparation for the Tribunal

Ray Newton agreed to help and they began detailed preparation for the hearing. From the outset Ray took the role of 'devil's advocate'. He took them through a 'decision tree' of matters that would be tested at the Tribunal hearing.

- He probed and tested the Disciplinary Procedures that they had installed, looking for anything that Kempton's advisers could claim was unfair – or any inconsistency between his treatment and that of anyone else who had been disciplined.
- He assembled copies of all the documents that Kempton also had copies of and checked them through. (They had nothing from the 'other side' to look at.)
- He set them up to 'role-play' the Tribunal hearing, to help them anticipate the questions and challenges that they were likely to meet from both Tribunal members and the CAB representative.
- He counselled them about keeping calm and focusing on the facts under questioning, however unfair or irrelevant it might seem.
- He advised Peter in particular to restrain his natural loquacity and answer the questions put to him politely but briefly, keeping to the point at issue.

Ray concluded that they did have a good, strong, well-documented case – but that it wasn't unassailable.

> 'You have good procedures, so the other side will have plenty of written materials to challenge. Because you have procedures, they can challenge them step by step. If you didn't have procedures, they'd attack you for not having any – you're there to be shot at in either case.'

> 'The chances are that there will be nothing written to go at from Kempton. As I understand it, no one will act as a witness for him – so we can't challenge them either! They'll rely on him appearing as a 'wronged party', fired for a first – in his case, second – offence in an otherwise blameless career of more than 20 years! You picked on him because you were determined to get rid of him because the business is in trouble and you wanted to avoid hefty redundancy costs!'

> 'If you believe that there is any real merit in that view of his case – you'd better say so now, before we get to the Tribunal. We must have faith in our case as well as having all the documented evidence to prove your procedures will stand up to scrutiny. You need to be very sure of your grounds before taking the procedure beyond this stage.'

Peter and Jennifer were convinced both of the fairness of their case, and of the strength of the procedures that they had applied consistently to all their staff since taking over the organization.

Peter informed the ACAS representative accordingly and refused to change his mind despite further attempts at persuasion for him to offer an out of court settlement. That is not to say that he and Jennifer had no doubts whatever. They would far rather not have had to go through the Tribunal hearing at all.

'Frivolous and Vexatious Cases'

Ray then tried to have the claim 'struck out' on the grounds that:

- Kempton had no valid basis on which to make his claim
- he was pursuing his claim in a manner that was 'frivolous and vexatious' and effectively would waste the Tribunal's time and
- they would seek to recover their costs from him once his action had failed.

The Employment Tribunal regional office did not accept their reasoning and so the hearing was set to continue on the date set.

What Happened at the Tribunal

On the first occasion, precisely nothing happened. Their case was not heard that day because others were ahead in the queue, and a previous action already once postponed was allowed to take precedence. After hanging around for about three hours until told that there was no chance for that day, they went miserably home.

On the second occasion, they were informed of another date a few weeks ahead. As it happened, Ray could not make that date, because he already had arrangements for that week that could not be postponed. Peter wrote back to the regional office, explaining the problem and asking for a postponement. This was granted, as the grounds were reasonable, and so a third date was set.

Then it was a case of 'third time lucky', now several months after George Kempton's dismissal. The long delay shows how vital it is to take statements from witnesses and assemble written evidence – notes of meetings and so on – immediately at the time of the events. Memories are uncertain and, before a tribunal, you are testifying on oath. It is a great help to have accurate written back-up for your memory in a highly stressful situation – at the end of which you could be more than £50 000 out of pocket. This time, they did get on to the day's list, with the hearing beginning at around 11 a.m.

A Cautionary Tale

Their experience was not unusual. Pressure on the tribunals' time is so great, and the length of a hearing so unpredictable, that it is not unknown for hearings to be postponed. Another unfortunate 'respondent' was told on this same occasion that there wouldn't be time that day. He had closed his entire shop down for the day (several staff were appearing as witnesses) and was very concerned at losing another day's trading in the future, yet another irrecoverable cost to him. Eventually, the Tribunal chairman established through the court clerk that there was a chance for the case to be heard by another Tribunal that had had a cancellation. After consulting maps, the entire group left to take up the offer, heading for the middle of a large city more than forty miles away. This story is quoted to show how stressful, as well as costly, involvement with tribunals can be.

We now come at last to the Speedwell hearing. But first, let's have your prediction of the Tribunal's decision.

POINT FOR DISCUSSION BREAK

So, what do you think happened? Did the Tribunal find:

● in favour of Peter and Jennifer Lewes and Speedwell
● in favour of George Kempton?

If it went in George's favour, would you expect the Tribunal to have ordered

● re-instatement
● re-employment
● compensation, up to the maximum of £50 000?

Would you expect their decision to be unanimous, or by a majority in either direction? Then write down your prediction, with the reasoning that led to your conclusion.

The Tribunal Hearing

Without repeating all the information that you have already read, the salient points to emerge from the hearing were:

The Attack

● George Kempton's representative handed Ray one sheet of paper just prior to the hearing. It was a general character reference provided by his 'employer before last' at Speedwell and so at least five years out of date. The gentleman who wrote it had, when Peter met him at a local function, expressed surprise that Kempton had not been sent 'down the road' as he put it, years ago. The document was never referred to in court.
● The CAB representative did in fact attack their procedures. She objected to the witness statements having been typed for them by Peter (even though they had read and signed them), and to the fact that a few days had elapsed between his making notes of what they said and returning them for signature.
● She objected to Jennifer having taken the appeal against dismissal, implying that it was impossible for her to have given an impartial verdict.
● She implied that there was an 'ulterior motive' for Kempton's dismissal. She had heard, presumably from George, that Speedwell was in financial trouble and that ridding it of her client would remove an expensive potential redundancy payment from its liabilities. The grounds for his dismissal were a pretext to be rid of him, come what might.
● She said that Kempton, despite long service and a previously unblemished record, had been dismissed without being given reasonable time for improvement.
● She charged Peter with neglecting supervision of the organization, in effect by not being there on every working day and night. She challenged the version of the incidents shown by the written evidence, implying that it was a 'story' constructed

to suit his particular wish to dismiss her client without cost, connived at by other employees who bore a grudge against George.

- She stated that Peter had replaced George with a less competent, untrained individual.

The Defence

- As predicted, George Kempton, although appearing clean-shaven, dressed in a dark suit, white shirt and a tie, did not make a good impression. He brought no witnesses with him and his wife was not present. When asked by the chairman why he thought that none of his former colleagues was willing to testify on his behalf, he said, 'They were all against me, that's all I know.' Otherwise, he was very quiet. He gave monosyllabic answers to questions from Ray about his conduct on the day in question.
- He did not really deny what he had been accused of doing, but blamed other people for 'annoying' him. In particular, he blamed Anne Chester, repeating that women had no place in production situations. Ray pointed out that Anne had to be persuaded by Peter not to quit her job over Kempton's continued harassment of her. Had he not persuaded her, she might have tried taking him to a tribunal herself, claiming Constructive Dismissal and possibly Sex Discrimination. If Kempton felt he had a genuine complaint against her, he could have used the Grievance Procedure set out in his Contract of Employment.
- Ray explained that Peter had in fact 'given George Kempton a chance to improve'. The first offence he had committed also amounted to Gross Industrial Misconduct, for which he could have been dismissed summarily. However, because both his previous employers had not provided records of any previous misdemeanours, Peter had shown clemency on the first occasion, by issuing a final written warning. However, when Kempton committed a further, related offence well inside the 'improvement period' provided for in the final warning, he believed it essential to dismiss Kempton.
- Peter explained that it was impossible to supervise Speedwell personally the whole time. To do so would involve his being there six days a week for up to eighteen hours a day. Since there were three separate activities – production, retail sales and wholesale sales (with more than twenty customers spread over a five-mile radius of the site) – even then it would be impossible to give full attention to George and his colleagues as well as to the retail staff and the delivery driver. The 'autonomous working group' system introduced by him with additional payment – and agreed to by all production workers including George – was put in place precisely to provide a sensible working framework.

In response to the other points made:

- Ray pointed out that, in a small organization, it was impossible to have a completely independent person to hear appeals. There were precedents, even in larger organizations, for a local site manager to hear appeals, so long as he or she was not directly involved in the disciplinary action and dismissal.
- Peter stated that the employee who had replaced George had precisely the same formal qualifications as George had himself. That was none, save for the Basic Certificate in Food Hygiene. He was paid the same rate as George had been paid. George's replacement showed that his dismissal was not an undeclared redundancy.

 REPRODUCED FROM *HOW TO AVOID EMPLOYMENT TRIBUNALS*, COLIN EVERSON, GOWER, ALDERSHOT

- Peter pointed out that if the hospital contract had been lost through Kempton's unacceptable hygiene standards, then the organization would certainly have been in serious trouble financially and could have lost its entire reputation locally as news spread.

POINT FOR DISCUSSION BREAK

Have you changed your mind about the probable verdict, having read this summary of the proceedings? If so, what has influenced you to do so?

It was very helpful to Peter to have someone else available to question George Kempton. It is a relevant point for anyone facing a former employee in a tribunal. There is always a risk that personalities will clash and the facts on which a dismissal was made will be obscured by rancour between the parties.

The Verdict

The Chairman brought proceedings to a conclusion, and then said that the Tribunal would announce its decision 'immediately after lunch'. Thus, Ray, Peter and Jennifer had another stressful hour to wait. Whatever the tribunal members had for lunch, the respondents were certainly left in turmoil. This is mentioned just to emphasize that facing tribunals is a very stressful matter, so be prepared to 'face the music' if you ever get involved with one.

At least when the verdict came, it did not take long to deliver. The Chairman stated simply that, on the 'balance of probabilities', they found that George Kempton had been fairly dismissed. They had done so by a majority verdict. One member of the Tribunal had felt that, though Kempton's offence was a grave one, he might have been allowed one more warning before he was dismissed.

Jennifer, Ray and Peter had not eaten any lunch. They now went off to a local tea shop for some 'comfort food' and a chance to relax before starting on the drive home.

FINAL POINTS FOR DISCUSSION BREAK

Did the Tribunal decision confirm your own opinion of the case?	Yes/No
Were you surprised that the verdict was by a majority?	Yes/No
Do you believe that the verdict was reasonable in the circumstances and with the evidence presented by the two parties?	Yes/No
Had Peter been required to prove that his assessment of George Kempton's conduct was fair 'beyond reasonable doubt', as in a criminal court, do you think that the Tribunal's verdict would have been different?	Yes/No

If so, why do you think it would, or would not, have been different?

Now, make any notes you believe appropriate to help you improve your own employment procedures to ensure that your organization can prove it behaves fairly if called upon to do so before an employment tribunal.

Notes:

 REPRODUCED FROM *HOW TO AVOID EMPLOYMENT TRIBUNALS*, COLIN EVERSON, GOWER, ALDERSHOT

Case study 2

AN APPLICATION REGARDING CONSTRUCTIVE DISMISSAL AND RACE DISCRIMINATION

Ranjit Singh, The Amalgamated Trade Union and the Commission for Racial Equality vs. *Sedgefield Distribution Ltd*

INTRODUCTION

This case study focuses on the difficult area of 'Constructive Dismissal'. An employee has not actually been dismissed, but has 'resigned' on the basis that it is impossible for them to continue working because the employer has made it impossible for them to do so. Read it carefully and use the discussion break points provided to review your own thoughts and opinions of the way in which the case progressed and was conducted.

An application regarding Constructive Dismissal and Race Discrimination

Ranjit Singh, The Amalgamated Trade Union and the Commission for Racial Equality vs. *Sedgefield Distribution Ltd*

PROCEDURAL CHECKLIST

A blank copy of the checklist is provided in Appendix 2 on page 93, which you can use as a check on the procedures of your own organization.

TRIBUNAL PROCEDURES

When you have read through the case, you may find it helpful to look at Tribunal Procedures on page 70, where there are charts showing the logic that is used to determine whether there has been Direct or Indirect Racial Discrimination.

THE GENERAL SCENARIO AT SEDGEFIELD'S DISTRIBUTION DEPOT

Ranjit Singh had worked for six years in a large depot for Sedgefield, a national distribution company. He had recently become a Team Leader for a section that picked items from the storage racking, in accord with the day's orders. His section assembled orders in the loading area, from which drivers loaded their own vehicles early the following morning. The workforce was predominately white; there were three loaders of West Indian descent, one of them in Ranjit's team. Ranjit was the only Sikh in the warehouse, though there were others working in other departments.

Sedgefield Ltd recognized a trade union acting for employees on all its sites. There was no closed shop agreement in force, but Ranjit was a member of the union. For some time now, because of long-term sickness, there had not been a permanent shop steward available for consultation on the site at which Ranjit worked.

All permanent employees were issued with a Contract of Employment and written Terms and Conditions of Employment. The site stated in policy documents and job advertisements that it was an 'equal opportunity employer'.

Tuesday Evening

Ranjit was responsible for a team of five loaders, excluding himself, working an afternoon shift running on this day, Tuesday, from 1 p.m. until 9 p.m., with a half-hour break at 6 p.m. The loaders used a mixture of hand-operated pallet trucks and fork-lift reach trucks to 'pick' the items, depending on where they were stored.

There were five other teams in the warehouse, doing similar work, all under the control of a First Line Manager, George Warwick. One other team worked the same hours as Ranjit. The other four teams worked to each of two slightly different shift patterns, providing cover from midday to 10 or 10.30 p.m., according to how much work had to be completed. Two teams took their breaks at any one time, so that there was always activity in the warehouse and the small tea room did not become overcrowded. The patterns changed over a three-week cycle, so that no one had a permanent late finish. Saturday was a normal working day, but the work was done in the morning ready for Monday, there being no deliveries made on Sundays. Sedgefield had a relatively high staff turnover, partly, it was thought, because of the permanently rather unsocial hours.

Wednesday Morning

The following day, Wednesday, Ranjit did not appear for work as usual. A telephone message from his brother later in the afternoon stated that 'Ranjit could no longer stand working for the company and he would not be returning to work, ever.' Ranjit's brother arranged to collect personal belongings from his locker. Since the company believed that he had in effect resigned without giving due notice under his contract, they only paid into his bank the amount that they owed him immediately up until the date of his employment ending.

Some Weeks Later

A few weeks later, Sedgefield was summoned to appear before an employment tribunal. Ranjit had filed an IT1 form, stating that he had been 'Constructively Dismissed'. He cited Racial Discrimination as the reason for his being forced to leave his employment. He had won support for his claim both from his union at regional level and from the Commission for Racial Equality.

It was company policy to contest all claims for Unfair Dismissal. On average, they 'won' about half of the cases – amounting to ten over the past six years – in which they appeared.

POINT FOR DISCUSSION BREAK

What do you think of the way in which Sedgefield's handled Ranjit Singh's departure from their company? Use the following points to clarify how you might have acted.

- Underline the word which you believe most closely describes their actions:

Inadequate   Cursory   Reasonable   Adequate   Thorough

- Would you have done anything differently, in the matter of:
  - investigating the circumstances surrounding his departure
  - the final payment that they made to him?
- Ranjit had worked for the company for six years. Would you have treated his departure differently had he been there for six weeks or sixteen years?
- Would his union membership have made any difference to how you acted? If so, what would you have done differently, and why?
- Are you surprised that he made an application to the employment tribunal?

YES/NO

- If you are not surprised, state why not.

SEDGEFIELD'S INVESTIGATIONS AND PREPARATION FOR THE TRIBUNAL HEARING

George Warwick prepared the company's case, which he discussed with the solicitor – who would represent them at the tribunal hearing – and the site General Manager.

Disciplinary Record

George's investigations revealed that there were three warnings shown on Ranjit Singh's personal file:

- a recorded Verbal Warning, given five years ago, for being late for work twice in a week
- a First Written Warning, given four years ago, for not appearing at work on a Saturday morning
- another First Written Warning, given two and a half years ago, for an argument with another employee (who left the company a few months later). Ranjit Singh had claimed the other employee, Sheila Wye, had made racist remarks to him, calling him a 'skiving, good-for-nothing Paki' and had levelled other racist insults at him. Sheila denied having called him names, but said he had often been late for work and that was why she told him he was 'lazy'. Though there were no witnesses to the original incident, several people saw and heard the subsequent quarrel. There being no direct witnesses to the initial cause of the row, both protagonists were reprimanded and issued with a First Written Warning.

There was nothing further concerning discipline on Ranjit's file and he had eventually been promoted about three months previously to Team Leader. As such, he would be assessed on an annual appraisal basis, but this had not happened yet because of the recent date of his promotion. He was due to attend a basic supervisory course a few weeks after he actually left the company.

Grievance Record

Ranjit had made a complaint through Sedgefield's Grievance Procedure about one month after being promoted. The grievance form he completed was short on detail. The kernel of his grievance seemed to be that his team resented him being 'promoted over them' and some of the other Team Leaders did not like working with him. There was a suggestion that this was because of his race, but no one was mentioned by name. Ranjit also said the others called him by a nickname that he took exception to, but he did not want to say what it was.

George had carried out the initial investigation, but found nothing of substance to get hold of. Staff were unwilling to talk much about the matter and 'pooh-poohed' the idea that there was any racial prejudice against Ranjit. They pointed out that Denzil Pyne-Bailey, a West Indian by descent, had worked with them for years and was a popular member of the team. Denzil was rather 'cagey' in his replies but, since he handed in his notice a couple of weeks later, George thought with hindsight that this was because he was already more interested in his new job.

George told Ranjit Singh that he could find nothing to substantiate his grievance. He offered him the chance to take it to the General Manager (the next stage in the formal procedure), but Ranjit declined to do so, saying it would 'probably be a waste of time'.

Preparation for the Tribunal

In addition to checking through the personnel files, George questioned members of both Ranjit's team and other teams, but he gained no useful information. He was confronted by a wall of silence, not helped by the fact that Denzil Pyne-Bailey had also left the company.

The company's solicitor recommended that Sedgefield should take up ACAS's offer of arbitration, as he had advised in other cases. However, the site General Manager decided to follow its usual policy, believing that the applicant's 'less than exemplary' disciplinary record (as he put it) would 'undermine his credibility in court'.

 REPRODUCED FROM *HOW TO AVOID EMPLOYMENT TRIBUNALS*, COLIN EVERSON, GOWER, ALDERSHOT

POINT FOR DISCUSSION BREAK

Would you have done anything differently if you had been preparing a defence for Sedgefield? Check your reasoning by answering the following questions:

- Would you have accepted ACAS's offer of arbitration, possibly leading to an offer of an out of court settlement (the way in which more than 40 per cent of cases are settled)?
- What is your view of Ranjit Singh's disciplinary record and its relevance to the proceedings?
- Why do you think that George Warwick met a 'wall of silence' when he asked people to tell him their recollection of the events preceding Ranjit's sudden departure?
- Assuming it came to the tribunal, would you expect the case to be decided.
  - in favour of the appellant, Ranjit Singh
  - or in favour of the respondent, Sedgefield Ltd?

You might underline your prediction so that you can compare it later with what happened at the hearing.

WHAT HAPPENED AT THE TRIBUNAL HEARING

Witnesses and Written Evidence

The appellant was represented by a solicitor, acting on behalf of his union and the Commission for Racial Equality. They called two witnesses, Denzil Pyne-Bailey and Sheila Wye. They also entered a copy of the grievance form which he had completed, a preliminary notice of the basic supervisory course he had been due to attend, his Contract of Employment and his final pay slip.

The Company, also represented by a solicitor, called no witnesses in addition to George Warwick, but presented written evidence including Ranjit's Contract of Employment, showing the notice he was required to give, his disciplinary record and the grievance claim which they had investigated on his behalf.

The Case for the Company

Through their solicitor, the company argued that:

- Sedgefield Ltd was committed to being an Equal Opportunities Employer and had an excellent record in that respect.
- Ranjit Singh had left their employment of his own accord, without giving due notice under his contract of employment.
- He had absented himself from work on previous occasions, so the manner of his departure was not that surprising to them.
- All staff were treated equally under their procedures; Sheila Wye, the other party in the argument that led to one of his written warnings, also received a Written Warning.

- Despite his less than exemplary disciplinary record, they had promoted him into a responsible job.
- He had not given proper notice, as required by the Contract of Employment, which he had signed.
- They had paid all monies due to him up to the time at which he resigned without notice.
- They had not sought any recompense from him for failing to give notice.
- After leaving them, Ranjit had made no attempt to contact the company, sending his brother to collect his personal belongings. He would not speak to George Warwick on the telephone.
- They had investigated thoroughly the circumstances of his departure and found no evidence that it had been made impossible for him to continue his employment.
- They showed evidence of his previous Grievance and showed that it had been investigated thoroughly.
- Though his complaint had not been substantiated, he had been offered the opportunity to take it to the next stage, but he had declined to do so.

In conclusion, they believed Ranjit Singh had no grounds on which to claim that he had been Constructively Dismissed. He had left of his own volition and failed to give proper notice, or indeed any notice, as required by his contract. By doing so, he had caused inconvenience to his employer and unilaterally broken his contract with them.

POINT FOR DISCUSSION BREAK

How strongly do you believe that Sedgefield have made their case that Ranjit has no grounds on which to claim Constructive Dismissal due to Racial Discrimination? Underline your selection from the list that follows:

Very strongly   Strongly   Moderately   Weakly   Very weakly

Remember what the definition of Constructive Dismissal is, checking with the Glossary on page 82 if necessary. Then list the particular strengths and weaknesses of Sedgefield's case as you see them:

Strengths:

1
2
3
4
5

Weaknesses:

1
2
3
4
5

The Case for Ranjit Singh

On behalf of Ranjit Singh, it was argued by his solicitor that:

- He had been subject to racial abuse by a number of staff, including Sheila Wye, over a long period and the company had not taken his complaint seriously.
- He had not been given sufficient training when he was promoted and this left him vulnerable to further racial taunts from members of his team and other team leaders. Other people had been trained much more quickly when they had been promoted.
- The atmosphere in the rest room was particularly offensive, he was often subject to derisive remarks about his turban and his colour, and had been told that he should 'make their tea, as he came from where it grew'.
- He found the nickname 'randy Ranjit' commonly applied to him particularly offensive, but when he complained to management, nothing was done.
- George Warwick did not supervise the warehouse sufficiently closely. He never appeared on Saturday mornings, or after 5.30 p.m., which was when the worst racial abuse occurred. Nor did he ever go into the rest room.
- Ranjit found George Warwick 'remote' and 'daunting' to deal with; he seemed much more friendly with the established Team Leaders. They talked a lot about the local football team and fishing, in which Ranjit had no interest.
- He, Ranjit, had not thought it worth trying yet again to talk to him once he had resigned – he knew other people who had left and no one had bothered to ask them why.
- It was irrelevant that he had three disciplinary references on his file, since the incidents happened long ago and the warnings had long since ceased to have any 'life' left in them.
- The 'final straw' was on the Tuesday on which he departed for the final time. A local newspaper was taped to his locker, open at the jobs page with three lowly jobs ringed and the words 'jobs seeking Randy' scrawled against them. Later, when he entered the rest room at breaktime, he was abused by two of his team, who directed racist jibes at him and complained that he was making them work too hard. A page from *Asian Lovelies* magazine had been fastened to his locker. When he returned to work, the pallet truck that he normally used had disappeared (he found it later, outside in the rain) and the seat of the fork-lift reach truck he used doused in tea and coffee dregs, which made a filthy mess of his overall.

Ranjit's solicitor concluded by saying that Sedgefield's management had permitted blatant acts of racial abuse against a long-serving and loyal employee. Their conduct had made it impossible for him to continue working for the company. In an area of high unemployment, Ranjit had been unable to find another job, so being forced to leave Sedgefield had caused him substantial and sustained financial loss. He should be compensated, both for his financial losses and the illegal discrimination of which he had been a victim.

┌───┐

POINT FOR DISCUSSION BREAK

Now you have read the other side of the case, and before you look at the witness statements that follow, how strongly do you believe Ranjit's claim to be that he was Constructively Dismissed? Underline your selection from the list that follows:

Very strong   Strong   Moderate   Weak   Very weak

List the particular strengths and weaknesses of his case as you see them:

Strengths:

1
2
3
4
5

Weaknesses:

1
2
3
4
5

Now, read what the witnesses said and see how it affects your view of the case.

The Witnesses

George Warwick

George related almost exactly what you have already read about his investigations into both Ranjit's grievance complaint and his departure. When questioned by Ranjit's solicitor and members of the Tribunal, he confirmed the following:

- It was not their practice to conduct 'exit interviews' with staff members who left, and he pointed out that, in Ranjit's case, there would have been no opportunity to have done so anyway.
- He seldom worked on Saturday mornings or after 5.30 p.m. He started early in the mornings and so thought it reasonable to leave the evening work to be run by the Team Leaders, all of whom he spoke to every day. He denied that he was remote or unapproachable, or that he favoured other Team Leaders above Ranjit. He could see nothing wrong in talking to them about subjects in which he knew them to be interested.
- He did not go into the staff's rest room on principle, feeling that they should not be bothered by him when they were on their breaks.
- He had seen no evidence of the matters that Ranjit described as happening on his final day when he was on site early the following morning.

The following witnesses appeared for Ranjit Singh.

Denzil Pyne-Bailey

Denzil had left the company of his own volition about six weeks before Ranjit and just two weeks after the grievance procedure actioned by his team leader.

In response to questions from Ranjit's solicitor, he stated that he knew that Ranjit had been subject to various forms of abuse, notably name-calling and generally being made to feel 'out of things' because he was not interested in football.

Asked by Sedgefield's solicitor why he had not told George Warwick about this at the time, he replied, 'It didn't seem worth the hassle – if the company had really been interested, they would have known what the atmosphere was like anyway – George was never around when anything happened.'

He confirmed, in answer to another question from Ranjit's solicitor, that he had left himself shortly afterwards because he didn't like the working atmosphere in the depot. No one had asked him why he was leaving, but that was 'no different to anyone else who left the place.'

Sheila Wye

Sheila Wye's evidence was brief and dealt chiefly with the argument between herself and Ranjit Singh. Although she had denied any racial motivation at the time, she now accepted that she had used the abusive term that he had claimed. She now regretted it, but at the time she had been more impressionable and had taken her cue from other members of staff who said such things, mainly behind his back. She had left the depot because she did not find the place very pleasant to work in.

Asked by the company's solicitor why she had now had such a change of heart, she said that she lived near Ranjit and had heard about his having been 'driven out' of his job and 'being unable to find anything else.'

She felt he had been given a raw deal and that the company 'ought to have done more to find out what was really going on, especially on Saturday mornings and later on in the evenings, when the management never seemed to be around.'

As with Denzil, she said that no one had asked her why she was leaving Sedgefield.

POINT FOR DISCUSSION BREAK

Now you have read the three witnesses' evidence, has this changed your opinion as to the likely verdict? If so, before reading on to the actual conclusion reached by the Tribunal, please note why you have changed your mind.

Notes:

The Tribunal's Verdict

The Tribunal, after a half-hour absence, decided that Ranjit Singh had been Constructively Dismissed and that Sedgefield were guilty of Direct Racial Discrimination. They did so unanimously. The Chairman said that they had failed to provide a proper degree of supervision and so allowed racial discrimination to flourish and had not provided Ranjit with proper training for his new role in the difficult circumstances he faced.

She went on to say that they accepted Ranjit's statement about the events of the Tuesday evening. They were in keeping with the picture which emerged from the evidence of a company in which racial prejudice was widespread and occasionally bubbled to the surface.

The Tribunal had considered making an order for Mr Singh's reinstatement, in view of his present unemployment. However, in view of the climate to which he would then return, they had instead decided to make a substantial award of compensation for Unfair Dismissal and Racial Discrimination.

FINAL POINT FOR DISCUSSION BREAK

Did the Tribunal decision confirm your own opinion of the case?　　　　YES/NO

Do you think it was reasonable in the circumstances and with the evidence presented by the two parties?　　　　YES/NO

Whichever answer you gave, compare the decision in this case with those given in actual cases by employment tribunals in Section 4. Is it in accord with the 'letter and spirit' of those decisions?　　　　YES/NO

Now, make any notes you believe appropriate to help you improve your own employment procedures to ensure that your organization
- treats people of all races fairly
- can prove it behaves fairly if called upon to do so before an employment tribunal.

Notes:

 REPRODUCED FROM *HOW TO AVOID EMPLOYMENT TRIBUNALS*, COLIN EVERSON, GOWER, ALDERSHOT

Case study 3

AN APPLICATION REGARDING UNFAIR DISMISSAL AND SEX DISCRIMINATION

Christine Wexford and the Equal Opportunities Commission vs. *Sandown IT Services Ltd*

INTRODUCTION

This case study focuses on the area of dismissal by reason of redundancy and a contention that the selection of a particular employee made redundant was unfair and discriminated against her because she was female. Read it carefully and use the break points provided to review your own thoughts and opinions of the way in which it progressed and was conducted.

An application regarding Unfair Dismissal and Sex Discrimination

Christine Wexford and the Equal Opportunities Commission vs. *Sandown IT Services Ltd*

PROCEDURAL CHECKLIST

A blank copy of the checklist is provided in Appendix 2 on page 93, which you can use as a check on the procedures of your own organization.

TRIBUNAL PROCEDURES

When you have read through the case, you may find it helpful to look at Tribunal Procedures on page 70, where there are charts showing the logic that is used to determine whether there has been Direct or Indirect Sex Discrimination.

THE GENERAL SCENARIO AT SANDOWN INFORMATION TECHNOLOGY SERVICES LTD.

Sandown had formerly been owned by a National Company, which had 'hived it off' three years previously, taking many of the existing staff – among them Christine Wexford – with it. All conditions of service were honoured by the new company, which now employed about one hundred and fifty staff. Sandown had a well-established appraisal system, linked to defined objectives for each coming year. All Sandown's personnel systems were what would be expected of a professionally run organization. Most records were held on computer and so were within the ambit of the Data Protection Act. No trade union was involved at the site.

At the time of her dismissal, Christine worked in a department that developed large-scale computer-based information systems. She had been doing so for five of her ten years service in total, having begun as a programmer when she joined direct from university. Her direct boss was Kevin Ripon, whom she had formerly worked alongside

REPRODUCED FROM *HOW TO AVOID EMPLOYMENT TRIBUNALS*, COLIN EVERSON, GOWER, ALDERSHOT

both as a programmer and in her present role of Systems Development Executive. He had worked for Sandown for around six years.

Some three weeks after Christine's annual appraisal interview, Sandown heard that they had lost the major contract to provide services to the former parent company. Since it represented a significant proportion of their business, it would affect employment prospects unless replacement business could be found quickly. Despite desperate efforts, this did not happen and redundancies became inevitable after a further two months. Christine was summoned by Kevin Ripon on a Monday morning, following a senior management meeting held over the weekend. She was shocked when he told her that she was to be made redundant. The dialogue set out here ensued:

Christine Wexford
'Am I the only one who is going – and why me anyway? Are you just getting rid of me because I'm female – am I the only woman they're getting rid of?'

Kevin Ripon
'No, you're not the only one. Five other people on your grade will be going – you understand there's nothing personal about it. It's simply that your jobs don't exist any more, because of the business that's gone. Redundancy is a perfectly fair reason to dismiss someone, regrettable though it is. In fact, you're not the only woman affected – I can't tell you the name as yet, but one other female is going from another department. It's a very sad business.'

Christine Wexford
'Not for you, Kevin – you'll still be here. It's me – and the others being sacked through no fault of their own – that it's sad for. Anyway, there are people here with nothing like as much service as me – we've always worked a "last in, first out" policy here. Not that it's happened all that often, but that's what the company has always done. There are two other people in my department on my grade with far less service – why not sack one of them? What reward do I get for my loyalty and hard work?'

Kevin Ripon
'There's nothing personal in this – it's simply a business decision for the good of the company overall. We'll do everything we can to help everyone find another job – we've been talking to a placement agency already. We'll pay you salary in lieu of notice and your state and company redundancy entitlement of course as well, exactly as your contract stipulates. We've never had an official "LIFO" policy – it was only custom and practice and we've never had so many jobs become redundant at the same time – remember it's the jobs that have become redundant, not the people.'

Christine Wexford
'It comes to the same thing from where I'm sitting. The fact is that I'm being thrown out after ten years' service and a good record of achievement and there are people with much less service who are being kept on. "LIFO" is a much fairer system – a lot of the so-called "other jobs" you talk of are with companies that think you're senile by the time you're thirty – the younger men would have a much better chance.'

 REPRODUCED FROM *HOW TO AVOID EMPLOYMENT TRIBUNALS*, COLIN EVERSON, GOWER, ALDERSHOT

Kevin Ripon

'You don't really know that at all. But it doesn't affect the issue for this company. We don't have a formal "LIFO" agreement, there's never been a union operating here who might have negotiated a binding company-wide agreement. And in any case, we would have reserved the right to maintain the requisite skill base within our human resource bank, "LIFO" or not. We don't do these things lightly and your case was debated fully and earnestly among all the others. Sadly, regrettably, your performance simply didn't place you amongst the bank of human resources essential to maintain the skill base I spoke of and so other criteria – like length of service – don't affect the argument.'

At this point, the conversation became heated and nothing substantial was said that would add to the record provided here. Christine duly cleared her desk, making sure she had copies of essential items such as appraisal records. She left the premises by the end of the week, not speaking formally to Kevin Ripon again before leaving. Her final settlement was duly paid into her bank account.

Two weeks later, Sandown received notice to appear before an employment tribunal. Christine had approached the Equal Opportunities Commission (EOC), who had agreed to take up her case – citing Unfair Dismissal, coupled with Sex Discrimination.

POINT FOR DISCUSSION BREAK

Taking the facts as presented, do you believe that Christine Wexford is likely to succeed in her claim? Make any notes that may be useful to you and re-assess your selection as further facts emerge. Underline your selection from the following choices:

Very likely to succeed
Fairly likely to succeed
50/50 chance of success
Unlikely to succeed
Very unlikely to succeed

Notes:

Sandown's Defence

The company decided to defend the case and rejected ACAS's offer of intervention. Mark Stratford, Kevin's immediate boss, and Sandown's Chief Executive, Nick Catterick, met one afternoon at the local golf course, to make sure they would not be interrupted. They were convinced they had a good case. It rested largely on the relative appraisal ratings of the three executives operating at the same level in Christine's former department. Both of the men she had mentioned as being younger and having less experience had appraisals that were marginally better than hers from a technical standpoint. They were also better qualified technically to do the job, in their Senior Managers' opinions. Added to that, was a 'rider' on Christine's appraisal, which is reproduced below:

> Christine, though a hard-working individual, is not always an ideal 'team player'. Her potentially explosive temperament, though normally well controlled, leads occasionally to a confrontational approach to colleagues and senior management. If Christine could control this unfortunate trait, she would increase her contribution to her team and the overall Sandown business substantially.

Ripon, Stratford and Catterick believed that this 'rider' was justified by the evidence of Kevin's final interview with Christine, at the end of which she had become very heated. Though there were no witnesses, evidence could be given on oath to that effect and her own testimony challenged as necessary by the company's solicitor.

There was also a recorded verbal warning on her personal file, following a dispute with Kevin about a year ago, concerning what she claimed were unreasonable performance criteria set out during her appraisal interview. In common with all the company's personnel records, it was held on computer as part of their drive for a 'paperless office'. Employees were provided with a paper copy and were required to sign their appraisal document in the presence of their appraising manager. The paper copy was then scanned into the personnel record held for the individual. At the request of Christine's solicitor, the company Human Resource Department made a copy of her most recent appraisal available to her.

Despite a further offer of intervention from ACAS, Sandown went ahead to tribunal, believing that they had a perfectly valid reason for dismissal through redundancy. No other employee had complained to a tribunal, which they felt strengthened their case, particularly as one of them was another woman, admittedly with much less service. Christine had received what they believed to be a handsome payoff, in accordance with her salary and length of service; they believed that she was simply 'chancing her arm' going to tribunal and had only a remote chance of winning her case.

┌───┐

POINT FOR DISCUSSION BREAK

Taking into account Christine's appraisal and the verbal warning she had also received, have you changed your mind about her chances of success at the tribunal? If you have changed your mind, please revise your selection from the original list of options, record it here and make a note of your reason for amending your prediction.

Amended selection (if appropriate)

Notes:

THE TRIBUNAL HEARING

Witnesses and written evidence

The appellant was represented by a solicitor, acting jointly on her behalf and that of the Equal Opportunities Commission. They called no witnesses.

The company, also represented by a solicitor, called no witnesses other than Kevin Ripon, but presented written evidence including Christine's appraisal and disciplinary record in printed format.

The Case for the Company

Through their solicitor, Sandown Ltd argued that:

- The company was committed to being an equal opportunities employer and had an excellent record in that respect, employing women in many management roles.
- Christine Wexford had been dismissed solely because her post had become redundant.
- She had been selected fairly, after a proper consideration of the company's future human resource requirements and need for a balanced skill bank.
- Other executives' posts, at the same level, had become redundant at the same time. They included a number of male employees as well as one other female.
- The company had followed its procedures fully. There was no written policy of 'last in, first out' as a criterion for selection for redundancy, nor was any such condition written into any employee's Contract of Employment. It had simply been 'custom and practice' in different circumstances.

- Christine's appraisal, which they would introduce as evidence, showed clearly that she was not as fitted, technically or temperamentally, as her two colleagues at equivalent level in her former department. The fact that they were both men was irrelevant; they met better the company's need for human resources during a difficult period.
- The evidence of the appraisal was borne out by the recorded verbal warning which had been issued to her in the preceding year.

No one else made redundant at the time had claimed that their dismissal was unfair, or was not the real reason for their dismissal.

In conclusion, they believed Christine Wexford had no grounds on which to claim that she had been unfairly selected for redundancy or had suffered discrimination on account of her sex.

POINT FOR DISCUSSION BREAK

How strongly do you believe that Sandown have made their case that Christine has no grounds on which to claim that she was unfairly dismissed, on the basis of the way in which her post was selected to become redundant and a victim of sex discrimination? Underline your selection from the list which follows:

Very strongly   Strongly   Moderately   Weakly   Very weakly

List the particular strengths and weaknesses of their case as you see them:

Strengths:

1
2
3
4
5

Weaknesses:

1
2
3
4
5

The Case for Christine Wexford

On behalf of Christine Wexford, it was argued by the EOC solicitor that she had been unfairly selected for redundancy and that

- she had been the victim of sex discrimination

 REPRODUCED FROM *HOW TO AVOID EMPLOYMENT TRIBUNALS*, COLIN EVERSON, GOWER, ALDERSHOT

- they would produce written evidence to prove that she had been unfairly treated under the company's appraisal system
- the Verbal Warning to which the company had referred was long out of time and referred to an incident involving a manager who apparently bore her a grudge
- there was in fact still time for other employees whose posts had been declared redundant to begin proceedings for Unfair Dismissal.

POINT FOR DISCUSSION BREAK

Now you have read the other side of the case, and before you look at the statements given in evidence that follow, how strong is your belief in Christine's claim that she was unfairly dismissed and a victim of sex discrimination? Underline your selection from the list that follows:

Very strong   Strong   Moderate   Weak   Very weak

List the particular strengths and weaknesses of her case as you see them.

Strengths:

1
2
3
4
5

Weaknesses:

1
2
3
4
5

Now, read what the witnesses said and see how this affects your view of the case.

The Verbal Evidence

The following witness appeared for Sandown Ltd.

Kevin Ripon

Kevin related almost exactly what you have already read about the company's way of deciding which posts must, regrettably, be declared redundant and the interview at which he had explained the facts, unpalatable though they must have been for her. The news had been equally unwelcome for the other staff affected. When questioned by Christine's solicitor and members of the tribunal, he stated that

REPRODUCED FROM *HOW TO AVOID EMPLOYMENT TRIBUNALS*, COLIN EVERSON, GOWER, ALDERSHOT

- he bore no animosity to her and that all the painful decisions had been taken purely on objective grounds and with the company's genuine business requirements in mind
- he had conducted Christine's appraisal and it had been confirmed by his own immediate boss, Mark Stratford, in line with standard procedures
- the 'custom and practice' to which Christine had referred in respect of selection criteria for dismissal when a post became redundant was not part of company policy. Custom and practice had not been intended to set a precedent and, in any case, this was the first occasion on which a number of posts had become redundant simultaneously.

Christine Wexford spoke for herself and stated that she believed she had been discriminated against for a number of years:

- She had been passed over for promotion in favour of Kevin Ripon and Mark Stratford, both of whom were involved directly in making her redundant. One of the two men on the same grade in her department, David Waterford, had been recruited by Mark and they were great golfing friends. They often played with both Mark Stratford and a less experienced employee, Peter Thurles, who had 'survived the carnage'. Christine did not play golf but, since they had never asked her whether she played, it would not have made any difference if she had.
- She had been unhappy for some time that Kevin conducted her appraisal. She believed that he had deliberately blocked her promotional path. This had ultimately led to the dispute with him over the previous year's appraisal and the 'recorded verbal warning' that she had believed at the time was unfair – the argument was a 'six of one, half-a-dozen of the other' affair, with Kevin losing his temper as much as she had over her lack of prospects for promotion.
- Now, in the form of the appraisal copy sent to her solicitor by the company's Human Resources Department, she had written proof. She had copies of both the appraisal that she had signed, and kept at home, and of the version retained in the company's computer files.
- The two versions were different. The 'rider' concerning her supposed temperament problem had been added after she had signed the document. She would not have signed it had she seen it but would instead have made a formal complaint to the Chief Executive, Nick Catterick.

Christine had also retained copies of eight previous appraisals. All of them showed that she had achieved more than satisfactory ratings and, so far as she could tell from them, had reached the business objectives set for her from year to year.

POINT FOR DISCUSSION BREAK

Now you have read the verbal evidence and the amended appraisal, have these changed your opinion as to the likely verdict? If so, note why you have changed your mind, before reading the actual conclusion reached by the Tribunal.

Notes:

 REPRODUCED FROM *HOW TO AVOID EMPLOYMENT TRIBUNALS*, COLIN EVERSON, GOWER, ALDERSHOT

The Tribunal's verdict

The Tribunal, after an hour's absence, decided that Christine Wexford had been dismissed unfairly and that Sandown were guilty also of Sex Discrimination. They did so unanimously. The Chairman said that:

- The Company had failed to show that they had selected Christine Wexford for redundancy fairly.
- The amendment to her appraisal, made without her knowledge after she had signed the original document, implied that there were undeclared reasons for selecting an experienced, able employee for redundancy ahead of less experienced colleagues in her department, both of them male.
- Coupled with the previous appraisals that the Tribunal had seen, mostly written by a manager other than Mr Ripon, this evidence presented a picture that contradicted the company's claim that she would not be able to make a contribution to their skill base equivalent to the two male colleagues retained in Mr Ripon's department.
- The verbal warning referred to was long out of time. They were inclined to accept Ms Wexford's account of the incident that led to it.
- The practice of having informal management meetings at a golf club, to which she was not invited but her junior male colleagues were, was redolent of a culture in which women were excluded from aspects of the management process.
- appraisals, showed her as an able, diligent employee over a number of years. Despite this, she had been overlooked for promotion on a number of occasions, each time being bypassed by male colleagues, two of whom were involved in her selection for redundancy.

The Tribunal had considered making an order for Ms Wexford's reinstatement. However, in view of the prejudicial climate to which she would then return, they had decided instead to make a substantial award for Unfair Dismissal and Sex Discrimination.

FINAL POINTS FOR DISCUSSION BREAK

Did the tribunal decision confirm your own opinion of the case?   Yes/No

Do you think it was reasonable in the circumstances and with the
evidence presented by the two parties?   Yes/No

Whichever answer you gave, please compare the decision in this case
with those given in actual cases by employment tribunals.
Is it in accord with the 'letter and spirit' of those decisions?   Yes/No

Now make any notes you believe appropriate to help you improve your own
employment procedures to ensure that your organization

- treats people of both sexes fairly
- can prove it behaves fairly if called upon to do so before an employment tribunal.

Notes:

Procedural checklist

Procedural Checklist
A Model to Compare With Your Own Practices

Questions	Notes	Model answer for Speedwell	Answers and actions for your organization		
			Yes/No	Action you will take	By Date
Are job vacancies advertised openly and are they open to people of either sex and any racial background to apply for?	Many organizations have an equal opportunities policy. What is essential is that they put it into practice.	Yes			
Does your organization deal with a recognized trade union that negotiates on behalf of its members with you?	If so, you will almost certainly have agreed Terms and Conditions of Employment for members with the union. Usually this will provide a sound framework for handling grievance and disciplinary issues.	Not applicable			
Does your organization provide formal induction training for new employees?	This is a good opportunity to get new employees off 'on the right foot', knowing exactly what you offer to them as an employer and what you expect of them as employees.	The Speedwell management had introduced induction training for new employees.			

REPRODUCED FROM *HOW TO AVOID EMPLOYMENT TRIBUNALS*, COLIN EVERSON, GOWER, ALDERSHOT

Questions	Notes	Model answer for Speedwell	Answers and actions for your organization		
			Yes/No	Action you will take	By Date
'Retrospective' induction	You should also think about 'retrospective' induction for existing employees missed for any reason, or who may have been inducted some time ago (the law and your requirements may both have moved on since).	Speedwell had not carried out retrospective induction, though they had introduced regular briefing sessions for all staff.			
Do you have an appraisal system or an equivalent system for agreeing objectives with employees and giving them objective feedback on their performance?	Fairly used, an appraisal system is an excellent way of managing employees, whatever their status. Records of appraisal interviews and achievements against agreed objectives should provide good evidence of fair, consistent management approaches.	No			
Have all employees been issued with a Contract of Employment and Written Terms and Conditions of Employment?	A legal requirement to be issued within two months of an employee's date of starting work. Smaller organizations employing less than twenty people are exempt from this requirement. However, it is good practice to do so anyway – fairer to employees and evidence of your own good faith and desire to be a reasonable employer.	Yes			

REPRODUCED FROM *HOW TO AVOID EMPLOYMENT TRIBUNALS*, COLIN EVERSON, GOWER, ALDERSHOT

Question	Guidance	Response			
	You need to look at the situation if you take over an existing organization, in case the previous owners had not complied with the law.				
Has the Contract been based on, or cross-referenced to, a model provided by, for example, your Trade Association, DTI leaflet PL 700 or the Chartered Institute of Personnel and Development?	Using a model document can save you time and ensure that you have access to the expertise and experience of organizations who work principally in the field of employment law.	Yes – in Speedwell's case, the Trade Association for their organization.			
Do the Terms and Conditions include a formal Grievance Procedure?	To be seen as fair, the Procedure should state clearly: • with whom an employee should raise a grievance in the first instance • the appeal procedure that the employee should follow if not satisfied with the initial response.	Yes			
Do the Terms and Conditions include a formal Disciplinary Procedure?	A normal, fair Procedure will include a number of stages: • Informal Warning or admonishment (not recorded) • First Written Warning • Second (and/or Final Warning) • Dismissal. It is prudent to keep a record in an employee's personal file of all warnings issued, with dates, and to require the employee to sign a copy to prove that (s)he is aware of the action taken. This includes 'Verbal Warnings' – if no written record is kept, how can you prove that it was issued?	Yes			

Questions	Notes	Model answer for Speedwell	Answers and actions for your organization		
			Yes/No	Action you will take	By Date
Do the Terms and Conditions state that an employee has the right to be accompanied by a colleague (or trade union representative if appropriate) in any disciplinary proceedings?	It is important, to be fair and seen to be fair, that the procedure is 'open' and that an employee cannot be pressured unduly by his or her boss 'behind closed doors'.	Yes – a colleague or appropriate member of staff according to the circumstances.			
Do the Disciplinary Procedures include provision for an 'improvement period'?	This relates to formal warnings. A reasonable period for a serious matter might be six months, after which the employee's performance will be re-assessed. 'Open-ended' warning periods will almost certainly be seen as unfair – you can't reasonably expect someone to work out a 'life sentence' for one offence.	Yes			
Do the Terms and Conditions spell out what will be seen as 'Gross (Industrial) Misconduct'?	You do not have to predict every possible situation. Gross (Industrial) Misconduct offences specified will often include: • fighting, 'horseplay' and unruly behaviour – including verbal abuse of work colleagues • major breaches of Health, Safety and Hygiene (legal or organizational requirements)	Yes			

 REPRODUCED FROM *HOW TO AVOID EMPLOYMENT TRIBUNALS*, COLIN EVERSON, GOWER, ALDERSHOT

• refusal to obey any reasonable instruction – for example, refusing to work with another employee because of their colour or gender • theft of, or malicious damage to the organization's property • illegal trading/disclosing trade secrets to a competitor. This is not a comprehensive list – it is impossible to envisage every situation which might arise in every organization. Common sense still has a part to play in deciding what constitutes Gross Misconduct.		
It is clear that Gross (Industrial) Misconduct will lead to 'Summary Dismissal'?	Yes	Summary Dismissal is a severe sanction, taking away benefits that may have accrued to an employee over a long period. It should only be used where the offence is so grave that he or she must be removed from the organization instantly.
Is it made clear that Summary Dismissal is Dismissal without Notice or any payment in lieu of notice?	Yes	It is fair and proper to ensure that employees know just what the penalty means – and what it will be imposed for – at the start of their employment with your organization.
Do the Terms and Conditions specify what sanctions other than dismissal may be imposed for breaches of discipline short of 'Gross Industrial Misconduct'?	Yes. In the Speedwell case, Kempton's offence did constitute Gross Industrial Misconduct. Their Terms and Conditions did not envisage suspension (with or without pay) as a possible sanction.	These might include: • demotion • suspension (with or without pay) for specified periods • specified 'fines' from wages (subject to any maximum legal limits in force) • Dismissal with Notice as set out in the Contract and subject to employment law.

REPRODUCED FROM *HOW TO AVOID EMPLOYMENT TRIBUNALS*, COLIN EVERSON, GOWER, ALDERSHOT

| | | Answers and actions for your organization | | |
Questions	Notes	Model answer for Speedwell	Yes/No	Action you will take	By Date
Have you talked through these provisions with each employee individually, to ensure that they understand the rules by which they must abide?	It is good practice, and demonstrably fair, to take a little time to go through the rules, bearing in mind that some employees will have little experience of legally binding contracts.	Yes			
Has every employee signed a copy of their Contract which you have retained on their personal file?	This will be good evidence that you have issued the documents. The signature shows that the employee has had the chance to read them and query anything that they do not understand, or which they believe is unfair.	Yes			
Have any changes been made to the Terms and Conditions since the Contract was issued initially?	Changes should not be imposed without the consent of all employees affected.	Yes			
Have these been discussed with, and accepted by, the employee(s) affected?	If changes are imposed unilaterally, employees may claim Constructive Dismissal before an employment tribunal.	Yes. Changes in working arrangements following redundancy of the Production Manager's post were discussed and agreed with all staff affected.			

 REPRODUCED FROM *HOW TO AVOID EMPLOYMENT TRIBUNALS*, COLIN EVERSON, GOWER, ALDERSHOT

Do you use standard documents for issuing written warnings?	Yes	These can be very helpful, saving time and ensuring that you deal consistently with all employees across every department. Model documents are available from Trade Associations and organizations like ACAS.		
Do you always provide a 'written statement of reasons for dismissal'?	Yes	This is a legal obligation for employees dismissed after 26 weeks' employment. However, it is good practice to do so for any employee. Failure to do so may strengthen an employee's case if a claim is made to an employment tribunal.		

REPRODUCED FROM *HOW TO AVOID EMPLOYMENT TRIBUNALS*, COLIN EVERSON, GOWER, ALDERSHOT

Tribunal procedures

THE 'ORDER OF RUNNING'

If you should eventually go to a tribunal, then you will begin the proceedings by responding to the appellant's complaint. You may call witnesses and produce written evidence to support your case. You will have sight of any written evidence to be produced by the appellant and they will have sight of yours. Important points to note are that

- all proceedings at the tribunal are conducted under oath – you must swear to tell 'the truth, the whole truth and nothing but the truth', just as you would in a court of law
- the tribunal will comprise a lawyer, who always takes the chair, sitting with two lay people who have a variety of industrial, commercial and industrial relations experience.

PRESENTING YOUR CASE

Neither side is compelled to be represented by a lawyer; it is permissible to present your own case. However, it is advisable to have someone to speak on your behalf:

- This may be a barrister or solicitor, but it does not have to be. You can choose to be represented by someone else, who speaks as a 'friend' on your behalf.
- This could be someone known to you who has experience of employment law, for instance a personnel manager, or simply someone who knows the facts of the case and its background well and who can speak independently and with authority on your behalf.

It is not advisable to conduct your own case, because

- you may be too close to it to 'tell the wood from the trees'
- emotion may cloud your judgement and prevent you presenting your case objectively
- you could become involved in a direct dispute with the appellant, should he or she decide also to present their case personally, and the word of one person against another is always fraught with risk.

Questions

You may be asked questions both by the appellant's representative and by members of the tribunal. Try to answer them unemotionally, keeping to the facts and avoiding 'value judgements' concerning the appellant's (or witnesses) character or motivation – they won't help your case and may well detract from it! Remember always that you are speaking on oath and must tell the truth to the best of your ability.

Briefing your representative – 'no surprises in court'

Assuming that you do have someone to represent you, then brief that person *thoroughly* and *honestly*, in advance of proceedings in which you will be speaking on oath. Whatever you do, don't hide anything from them that might emerge at the tribunal. Your representative must be aware of the strengths and weaknesses of your case before the event.

Never underestimate the abilities of the tribunal members. They have a wealth of experience of both employment law and of what happens in the' real world' of business.

Case studies

Study those aspects of the three case studies in this Resource that demonstrate how things can go wrong through inadequate preparation. Remember that the 'other side' is just as anxious to win as you are – and they have the incentive of a potentially large award, whereas you will almost never be in a position to recover anything financially from them.

Role-playing

You could practise role-playing by taking one of the three cases described in detail in this resource. Sufficient information is provided about the main characters in each of them for you to select three or four of them from whichever case is most relevant to your own circumstances.

It makes sense to set up a role-play of your own tribunal hearing as you anticipate it will happen. Your representative could present the other side's case, or play 'devil's advocate' to test any weaknesses in your case. There are some important points to consider:

- This can be an uncomfortable experience for you both – don't go into it thinking otherwise.
- Friendships can be put under strain, especially if your case really has weaknesses in it.
- If your representative can see the weaknesses, the appellant's representative will obviously be able to exploit them. It is better to know in advance.

Arbitration

Pride is a poor reason for going to court, and can be very expensive. If your study of the case studies given compared with your own circumstances, your representative's analysis of your case, or the outcome of the role-play you conduct suggest that your case is weak and not likely to succeed, then you will be well advised to consider ACAS's offer of arbitration. This may well be a cheaper option than losing at a tribunal – you only have to look at the awards made that are quoted in this Resource.

Written materials

It is very helpful – in reality essential – for you as an employer to present written evidence, such as:

- Contracts of Employment /written Terms and Conditions of Employment
- written statement of reasons for dismissal
- organization handbooks, records of training, records of relevant briefing meetings
- records of appraisals
- records of all current disciplinary actions and formal grievance investigations relevant to the case
- records of disciplinary appeal procedures
- signed witness statements
- policy statements covering, for example, opportunities, health and safety, recruitment practices.

If you don't have any written evidence, you may have acted perfectly fairly and still lose your case on procedural grounds. The risk isn't worth taking. However, do try to keep the paperwork presented down to that which is essential and relevant to the specific case, as this will help the tribunal members. Don't be surprised if the appellant provides very little paperwork to support his or her case.

Tribunals are often held long after the events they refer to. Memories can be hazy, or clouded by emotions, which is another good reason for having supporting written evidence to back up your oral evidence.

Practising what you preach

Remember, having policies is no use unless you put them into practice. If you have policies and do not implement them, you're probably going to be worse off than if you have none. Policies can be like a millstone around your neck if the other side can show that you either don't implement them at all or don't implement them consistently between employees or classes of employees.

Fairness

The tribunal will look to you to show that you have applied your policies fairly, between individual employees and between classes or groups of employees. To demonstrate this, you need to have applied your policies with reasonable consistency and not favoured a particular group or individual over issues such as promotion or treated an individual or group less favourably over an issue such as selection for redundancy.

The main grounds for appealing to a tribunal

Frequent reasons for appealing to a tribunal are:

- Unfair Dismissal/Constructive Dismissal
- Direct Sex Discrimination
- Direct Race Discrimination
- Indirect Discrimination on the grounds of sex or race
- Victimization.

Not infrequently, an appellant will cite more than one of these grounds in the application, perhaps coupling Unfair Dismissal with Sex or Race Discrimination.

Use of Glossary

Please refer to the Glossary provided with this Resource to check the meaning of any unfamiliar terms used in this chapter, or words that have been assigned a specific meaning within the law. For example, 'requirement or condition', 'comparator', 'protected act', 'reinstatement', 're-engagement'.

What the tribunal will look for

Dismissal must *normally* be made for one of a number of specific reasons to be regarded as fair within the law. The normally admissible reasons are:

- misconduct
- inadequate qualifications or capabilities (including health)
- redundancy (of the *job* carried out by the employee dismissed)
- compliance by the employer with a legal requirement (for example, not holding an appropriate type of licence to operate a vehicle, aircraft or ship)
- some other substantial reason.

In each case, the tribunal will ask itself a series of questions to test whether the applicant has a valid case against the former employer.

Warning note

The four charts that you are about to look at should convince you of the thoroughness with which a tribunal will investigate every applicant's complaint against an employer. The tests applied are logical and in general don't leave room for 'waffle' or dissembling from either party. Tribunal members receive training and updating in tribunal procedures and employment law as changes occur. The charts are included to:

- convince you that you must have a good case to succeed at tribunal
- demonstrate that you must be able to substantiate your actions, however fair you may believe that they were
- convince you not to get into the situation of appearing before a tribunal unless you are convinced that you should win.

Unfair Dismissal

Question		Action if answer 'yes'	Action if answer 'no'
1 Is the applicant within their rights to complain?	Yes/ No	Go to question 2	**Complaint is dismissed** Tribunal will find for the employer
2 Does the applicant still retain the right to complain?	Yes/ No	Go to question 3	**Complaint is dismissed** Tribunal will find for the employer
3 Did the employer dismiss the applicant?	Yes/ No	Go to question 5	Go to question 4
4 Did the applicant resign as a result of the employer breaching their contract?	Yes/ No	Go to question 5	**Complaint is dismissed** Tribunal will find for the employer
5 Can the applicant demonstrate that the reason for dismissal was 'automatically unfair'?	Yes/ No	**Complaint succeeds** Go to question 11	Go to question 6
6 Has the employer ('respondent') failed to show the reason for dismissal?	Yes/ No	**Complaint succeeds** Go to question 11	Go to question 7
7 Could the reason for dismissal not be regarded as fair?	Yes/ No	**Complaint succeeds** Go to question 11	Go to question 8
8 Was the way the dismissal was made unfair from a procedural point of view?	Yes/ No	**Complaint succeeds** Assess the % chance (on a scale of 0 to 100) that the applicant could have been dismissed fairly. Then: go to question 10	Go to question 9
9 Was dismissal an unreasonable response to the offence?	Yes/ No	**Complaint succeeds** Go to question 10	**Complaint is dismissed** Tribunal will find for the employer
10 Did the applicant's conduct contribute to their dismissal?	Yes/ No	Assess applicant's % contribution on scale of 0 to 100.	Go to question 11
11 Would reinstatement be an appropriate remedy?	Yes/ No	**Order employer to reinstate employee**	Go to question 12
12 Would re-engagement be an appropriate remedy?	Yes/ No	**Order employer to re-engage the employee**	Go to question 13
13 Would compensation be an appropriate remedy?	Yes/ No	**Decide level of compensation using standard formula** Take account of employee's % contribution to the dismissal, if any.	

 REPRODUCED FROM *HOW TO AVOID EMPLOYMENT TRIBUNALS*, COLIN EVERSON, GOWER, ALDERSHOT

Direct Sex or Race Discrimination

Question		Action if answer 'yes'	Action if answer 'no'
1 Has the applicant been treated less favourably than • a real 'comparator' • a hypothetical 'comparator'?	Yes/No	Go to question 2	**Complaint fails**
2 Is the 'comparator' • of the opposite sex • of different marital status • from a different racial group?	Yes/No	Go to question 3	**Complaint fails**
3 Has the respondent failed to explain the reasons for the less favourable treatment?	Yes/No	**Complaint succeeds** Go to Box 9	Go to question 4
4 Is the complaint on the basis of Sex Discrimination?	Yes/No	Go to question 5	It is therefore about Race Discrimination. Go to question 6
5 (Sex Discrimination) Do you find the explanation (question 3) inadequate or unsatisfactory?	Yes/No	**Complaint succeeds** Go to Box 9	**Complaint fails**
6 (Race Discrimination) Do you find the explanation (question 3) inadequate or unsatisfactory?	Yes/No	Go to question 7	**Complaint fails**
7 Are you prepared to infer that there has been discrimination?	Yes/No	**Complaint succeeds** Go to Box 9	Go to question 8
8 Is your decision not to infer discrimination not justifiable on rational grounds?	Yes/No	**Complaint succeeds** Go to Box 9	**Complaint fails**
	Box 9	Implement Remedy: 1 Declaration of rights 2 Compensation for: • loss of earnings • injury to feelings • damages for personal injury 3 Interest 4 Other recommendation, as appropriate.	

Indirect discrimination on the grounds of sex or race

Question		Action if answer 'yes'	Action if answer 'no'
1 Has the respondent imposed a requirement or condition?	Yes/No	Go to question 2	**Complaint fails**
2 Does the requirement or condition apply equally to people *not* of the applicant's race or sex?	Yes/No	1 Identify the pool of people who can comply with the requirements or conditions imposed **excluding** the one with which the applicant cannot comply 2 Within that pool, identify all those who can comply with all the requirements or conditions **including** the one with which the applicant cannot comply Then: go to question 4	Go to question 3
3 Is there any evidence of Direct Discrimination?	Yes/No	Go to previous table covering Direct Sex or Race Discrimination	**Complaint fails**
4 Is the proportion of people of the applicant's race or sex who can comply with the requirement considerably smaller than the proportion of people not of the applicant's race or sex who can comply?	Yes/No	1 Balance the discriminatory effect of the requirement or condition against the reasonable needs of the respondent's business. Then: go to question 5	**Complaint fails**
5 Has the respondent failed to justify the requirement or condition on objective grounds?	Yes/No	Go to question 6	**Complaint fails**
6 Is it impossible for the applicant to comply with the requirement or condition?	Yes/No	Go to question 7	**Complaint fails**
7 Is it to the applicant's detriment that he or she cannot comply?	Yes/No	**Complaint succeeds** Go to Box 8	**Complaint fails**
	Box 8	Implement Remedy: 1 Declaration of rights 2 Compensation for: • loss of earnings • injury to feelings • damages for personal injury 3 Interest 4 Other recommendation, as appropriate.	

 REPRODUCED FROM *HOW TO AVOID EMPLOYMENT TRIBUNALS*, COLIN EVERSON, GOWER, ALDERSHOT

Victimization

Question		Action if answer 'yes'	Action if answer 'no'
1 Has the applicant performed a 'protected act'?	Yes/ No	Go to question 2	**Complaint fails**
2 Has the applicant been treated less favourably than if he or she had not performed a 'protected act' by reference to a comparator?	Yes/ No	Note: The race and sex of the applicant and the comparator are irrelevant Go to question 3	**Complaint fails**
3 Was the less favourable treatment because the applicant had performed, or intended to perform, a 'protected act'?	Yes/ No	Go to question 4	**Complaint fails**
4 Was the applicant's allegation true *or* made in good faith?	Yes/ No	**Complaint succeeds** Go to Box 5	**Complaint fails**
	Box 5	Implement Remedy: 1 Declaration of rights 2 Compensation for: • loss of earnings • injury to feelings • damages for personal injury 3 Interest 4 Other recommendation, as appropriate.	

Glossary

Glossary

ACAS: Advisory,
Conciliation and Arbitration Service

The body that seeks to achieve a general improvement in industrial relations. ACAS is notified automatically of any claim of Unfair Dismissal and has a duty to try to obtain a settlement.

Admonishment

See 'Informal Warning'.

Applicant

The person who makes a claim to an employment tribunal.

Automatically Unfair Dismissal

Dismissal for a reason which is illegal, for example pregnancy; sex; race or religious grounds.

Balance of probabilities

The test applied by an industrial tribunal to test the reasonableness of an employer's decision.
See also 'Reasonableness of decision'.

Beyond reasonable doubt

The test applied in criminal courts, which is much harder to pass than the 'balance of probabilities' required by an employment tribunal. This is principally because a criminal court can deprive an individual of his or her liberty.

Burden of proof

See 'Reasonableness of decision'.

C.A.B.

See 'Citizens' Advice Bureau'.

Chairman (of employment tribunal)

A legally qualified individual is always appointed to chair a tribunal.

Citizens' Advice Bureau

The body to which any individual can turn for help and advice on almost any subject, including Unfair Dismissal. Will frequently represent appellants at employment tribunals at no cost to the individual.

Commission for Racial Equality

The principal body that deals with matters of race discrimination. The CRE may take up cases on behalf of an applicant to a tribunal where it believes that wider public issues of policy are involved.

Community Legal Service

A government sponsored initiative designed to 'ensure that everyone who needs it has access to good quality legal advice and information'. 'Unfair treatment at work' is one of the issues singled out in its advertising literature aimed at potential users.

Comparator	A real or hypothetical 'benchmark' against which the requirements imposed on an appellant claiming sex or race discrimination may be compared by an employment tribunal.
Compensation	The monetary award that may be made to an individual whose action for unfair dismissal on any grounds succeeds. Amounts awarded are calculated according to standard formulae and will vary according to the circumstances and reason for dismissal. (See 'Race Discrimination', 'Sex Discrimination', 'Unfair Dismissal').
Complaint to an employment tribunal	Can be made by any individual who believes that they have been dismissed unfairly, using a standard form obtainable from job centres and other offices concerned with employment.
Consistency	Often used as though it meant the same as 'fairness'. Consistency requires that the same sanction must be imposed for the same offence under any and every circumstance. For example, it would be 'consistent' under rules relating to Gross Misconduct to

- dismiss summarily an employee with one year's service for taking company property home without authorization
- dismiss summarily an employee with forty years' service one day before their retirement date for taking company property home without authorization.

The two decisions would be consistent, but would they both be fair? *See also* 'Fairness'.

Constructive dismissal	Occurs when something is changed so radically in an employee's Conditions of Employment – without their consent – that it amounts effectively to dismissal. For example, demoting someone from sales manager to delivery driver, or moving their place of employment 100 miles away from their present base without their consent could well be seen as Constructive Dismissal.
Contract of Employment	A document that sets out the main terms and conditions of the agreement between employer and employee.
Custom and practice	The recognized 'unwritten rules' by which organizations have operated over a period of time. They may be an unreliable foundation on which to build a case for dismissing an employee – written rules and procedures are much more easy to demonstrate.
Data Protection Act	The law that governs the storage and use of information about employees (among many other classes of data) and applies to all computerized records.

Disability Discrimination Act	The law that protects the rights of disabled people at work.
Disciplinary action	An action, or series of actions, taken by an employer against an employee who will not conform with the standards required by an organization and set out in their Contract and Terms and Conditions of Employment.
Disciplinary Procedure	A framework of procedures that is intended to help employers and employees conform to, or return to, agreed standards of conduct and performance. Most employees and employers will never breach them to any significant degree.
Employment Appeal Tribunal	The legal body to which appeals from an employment tribunal may be made, under defined conditions concerning its procedures.
Employment Protection Act	The Law which governs the general relationships between Employers and Employees.
Employment Tribunal (formerly Industrial Tribunal)	The legal body that can determine the merits of applications brought to it under the various laws affecting employment. Its decisions are legally binding. The three members comprise a chairman who is legally qualified, and two 'lay members', usually with industrial, commercial and/or trade union backgrounds.
Equal Opportunities Commission (EOC)	The principal body that deals with matters of Sex Discrimination. The EOC may take up cases on behalf of an applicant to a tribunal where it believes that wider public issues of policy are involved.
Fair reason for dismissal	*See* 'Reason for dismissal'.
Fairness	*See also* the example quoted under 'Consistency', with which it is often regarded as a synonym. In essence

- 'consistency' is objective and can be measured or demonstrated through factual evidence
- fairness is subjective and allows more scope for the circumstances of a case and an individual to be taken into account.

In the example given under 'Consistency', it might be thought fairer to 'turn a blind eye' to one offence committed on the eve of retirement after 40 years' blameless service but it would not be consistent with other decisions in 'less deserving' cases.

First Written Warning	The initial formal stage in most disciplinary procedures.
Form 1T1	The form that an applicant to an employment tribunal completes to initiate a tribunal hearing.

Friend	A person who, though not a practising lawyer, may represent an employee or employer before an employment tribunal.
Frivolous or vexatious action	An action which is so ill-founded that it should never have been brought and amounts to a waste of the tribunal's time and resources. In exceptional circumstances, it may lead to an award of costs against the applicant.
Grievance Procedure	The formal procedure through which an employee can raise matters that he or she believes are weighing upon them unfairly.
Gross (Industrial) Misconduct	This is conduct so flagrantly in breach of reasonable discipline that it 'goes to the root' of an employee's contract. The normal penalty is the severe one of Summary Dismissal. Examples include • theft, misuse or damage to property • fighting, horseplay, verbal abuse of colleagues • deliberate breaches of Health and Safety law • drunkenness • breach of confidentiality, e.g. giving sensitive information to a competitor.
Hearsay evidence	Evidence of conversations bearing on the alleged offence. For example, a working colleague of the applicant may claim to have heard the applicant telling a third party of an intention to steal property, or threaten another employee. Such evidence is admissible at a tribunal, but would not be in a criminal court.
Ignorance of the law	Saying you did not know a law existed, or did not understand it or that it applied to you is not a valid defence under United Kingdom law. The law demands that individuals check what law may apply before they take any action. Otherwise, it would be too simple for offenders to plead that they did not know it was illegal to fish in that river, light a coal fire in that town or drive at 120 mph – in fact, do anything that they desire without fear of legal sanction.
Improvement period	A reasonable period specified for an employee's conduct to improve (subject to review with the employer) following a formal Written Warning. The length of time specified should be proportionate to the offence and probably never longer than six months as a 'rule of thumb'.
Indirect Discrimination	This can be Racial or Sex Discrimination. It occurs when a condition is imposed that affects a person adversely because of their race or sex. For example: • demanding that every employee must have blue eyes would discriminate against almost all black people • demanding that every employee must be six feet tall would discriminate against most women.

There are some exceptions to the general principle, but check carefully if you think your conditions of employment may constitute a 'fair' exception.

Industrial Tribunal	*See* 'Employment Tribunal'.
Informal Warning	A verbal warning issued for a minor offence, prior to placing an employee in the organization's formal disciplinary procedure. Normally, no record of such warnings would be kept in an employee's file.
IT1	*See* 'Form IT1'.
Members (of employment tribunals)	*See* 'Employment tribunals'.
Misconduct	Breaches of disciplinary procedures that fall short of Gross (Industrial) Misconduct, and will be subject to lesser sanctions, such as demotion, loss of seniority, being denied promotion, or a Formal Warning subject to an improvement period.
Notice period	The notice required to be given by the employer to the employee and vice versa under the Contract of Employment agreed between them. Note that there are minimum legal provisions for notice that you should check when drafting contracts. In practice, employees frequently do not keep to the notice that they are required to give and it is unusual for employers to seek to enforce it.
Out of court settlement	A settlement agreed by both parties before a hearing comes before an employment tribunal. ACAS are often involved in helping to negotiate out of court settlements. Remember that entering into negotiations with an employer for an out of court settlement does not take away the employee's right to pursue a claim through the employment tribunal subsequently.
Potentially fair (reason for dismissal)	A test applied by an employment tribunal to check whether the reason to dismiss could be fair – for example, if it was one of the normally acceptable reasons for dismissal. *See also* Reasons for Dismissal.
Procedurally fair (or unfair)	A test applied by an employment tribunal to check that an employer has followed procedures as they are set out (for example, in discipline, grievance handling or selection for redundancy) before dismissing an employee.
Protected act	An act performed by an employee, on their own or another employee's behalf, in respect of which discrimination by the employer would automatically be regarded as Victimization. Examples could include

- asserting rights under the Sex Discrimination Act
- asserting rights under the Equal Pay Act
- giving information to a body such as the Equal Opportunities Commission (EOC).

Racial Discrimination	Discrimination against employees on the basis of their race is illegal. An employer found guilty of Racial Discrimination against an employee can face an unlimited award of compensation.
Reason for dismissal	Dismissal must *normally* be made for one of a number of specific reasons to be regarded as fair within the law. The reasons are

- misconduct
- inadequate qualifications or capabilities (including health)
- redundancy (of the *job* done by the employee dismissed)
- compliance by the employer with a legal requirement (for example, that the employee must hold an appropriate type of licence to operate a vehicle, aircraft or ship that the employee did not have)
- some other substantial reason.

Reasonable response	A test imposed by an employment tribunal to check whether dismissal was appropriate in the circumstances. For example, dismissing an employee summarily for a first minor offence (say, being ten minutes late for work after five years previously unblemished service) is unlikely to be considered a 'reasonable response'.
Reasonableness of decision (to dismiss)	An employer needs to show the tribunal that

- the dismissal was genuinely for the reason given and was not related to a hidden agenda
- the belief that an employee committed the offence was based on reasonable grounds, normally evidence that allows the employer to say that, on balance, it was more probable that the employee committed the offence than that they did not
- the belief was based on a reasonable investigation held before the dismissal took place. The investigation must include an opportunity for the employee to offer an explanation.

See also 'Balance of probabilities' and 'Beyond reasonable doubt'.

Recognized trade union	A legally certified independent trade union that an employer has recognized to hold negotiating rights on behalf of a group of their employees. Many people may be members of a union that does not have such rights, possibly because they no longer work in an industry with which their union is chiefly involved.
Record of disciplinary hearing	Based on notes made at the time. A record should be placed in the employee's personal file and provided to the employee as evidence that s/he has received a fair hearing.

Recorded Verbal Warning	A record in an employee's personal file of a Verbal Warning given as the first stage in the formal Disciplinary Procedure. The record will guard against lapses of memory should further stages in the procedure need to be invoked.
Redundancy	Redundancy in law applies to the *job* that an employee was doing and not the person doing it. It can be a valid reason for dismissal. For example, if reduced sales reduce the need for warehouse activity, then a number of posts for packers, loaders and fork-lift truck drivers may become redundant. The people who filled those posts could be re-deployed to other suitable jobs, should such be available.
	Any agreement as to selection criteria for redundancy must be observed, for example a 'last in, first out' (LIFO) agreement with employees or a recognized trade union, subject to any agreed provisions necessary to protect the skills base of the remaining organization.
Redundancy (as reason for dismissal)	Redundancy can be a valid reason for dismissal, but it is important to show that
	● the reason really was that the employee's post had become redundant ● redundancy was not a pretext for dismissing the employee for some entirely different, undeclared reason ● the former employee's post has not been refilled by another person doing the same work.
Re-engagement	A remedy available to an employment tribunal that has found an employee to have been dismissed unfairly. It requires the employer to re-employ the former employee, but not specifically in the job from which (s)he was dismissed. This is not so hard for an employer, especially a large organization, to implement as reinstatement.
Reinstatement	A remedy available to an employment tribunal that has found an employee to have been dismissed unfairly. It requires an employer to reinstate the employee to the former position and conditions of employment (for example, pension rights, salary) as though the dismissal had never taken place. In practice, this is an extremely difficult remedy for an employer to implement – almost certainly another employee has taken over the position. It is worth noting that if an employer refuses to reinstate the employee, then the tribunal will make a substantially higher award for compensation to the employee.
Remedies for unfair dismissal	*See* 'Compensation', 'Re-engagement', 'Reinstatement'.
Requirement or condition	*See* 'Indirect Discrimination'.
Respondent	The organization that has been accused at an employment tribunal of treating an employee unfairly in any respect.

Right to complain	You must have such a right to succeed as an applicant to an employment tribunal. The complaint must be made within a prescribed time, or the right will lapse. Some people are normally excluded, for example anyone over the state retirement age, people working on a fixed-term contract dismissed solely because the contract has ended. The time allowed and categories affected will change from time to time and you are advised to check with, for example, ACAS, the Citizens' Advice Bureau or your Trade Association if you are in any doubt about a specific circumstance.
Second Written Warning	The normal second stage in a formal disciplinary procedure, following which the next stage will be dismissal if no improvement is accepted to have been made within the stated 'improvement period'.
Sexual Discrimination	Discrimination against employees purely on the basis of their gender is illegal except under very exceptional circumstances (for example, some aspects of the armed forces). An employer found guilty of Sex Discrimination can face an unlimited award for compensation.
Summary Dismissal	Dismissal without notice or payment in lieu of notice. The employee forgoes all employment rights, for example accumulated holiday pay. Dismissal takes effect immediately and the employee leaves the employer's premises without delay. It is a severe sanction, reserved for offences which 'go to the root' of the employee's contract with the employer. *See also* 'Gross Misconduct'.
Terms and Conditions of Employment	A written statement of the main terms and conditions that govern an employee's employment, including those relating to disciplinary and grievance procedures.
Trade Union Activity (dismissal for)	It is normally automatically unfair to dismiss an employee for legitimate trade union activity.
Unfair Dismissal	Dismissal of an employee by an employer without a justifiable reason and/or contrary to the law.
Verbal Warning	Normally the first formal stage in a disciplinary procedure. It is prudent to record all such warnings, just in case the recipient forgets them prior to later stages in the procedure.
Vexatious or frivolous action	*See* 'Frivolous or vexatious action'.
Written statement of reasons for dismissal	A document that must be issued to a dismissed employee, setting out the reasons for his or her dismissal. Failure to do so may prejudice the employer's case before an employment tribunal.

Appendices

 **Appendix 1**

Personal Attitude Questionnaire

Question Number	Statement	Your rating 1 strongly disagree 2 tend to disagree 3 open to persuasion 4 tend to agree 5 strongly agree				
		1	2	3	4	5
1	I believe it is a manager's right to manage and the law shouldn't interfere with how I manage people.					
2	Employees have had a hard time from employers for too long now – it's time something was done to tilt the balance in their favour.					
3	Paperwork systems are a waste of time – managers have better things to do with their time.					
4	Employment tribunals don't affect smaller organizations.					
5	We can run our organization on the basis of mutual trust – we don't need loads of systems to help us get on together.					
6	Once the management has decided to get rid of someone, there's nothing an employee or the law can do about it, providing you've got watertight systems in place.					
7	The law doesn't expect smaller organizations to keep records like the bigger ones do – they haven't the time or the need.					
8	Employees caught stealing should be sacked immediately – it doesn't matter if they've been there 20 minutes or 20 years.					
9	Induction Training is essential to let people know where they stand from day one.					
10	Doing everything by the book means you can get rid of anyone you need to, without any comeback – that's what the systems are for.					
11	Briefing sessions for employees are just an excuse for them to stop working and gripe about their jobs. I'll soon tell them if they don't come up to scratch.					
12	You should make allowance for employees' individual circumstances when deciding on disciplinary action.					
	Your totals					

Appendix 2

Procedural Checklist:
A Model to Compare with Your Own Practices

Page 1 of 4

Question	Notes	Yes/No	Action you will take	By Date
Are job vacancies advertised openly and are they open to people of either sex and any racial background to apply for?	Many organizations have an equal opportunities policy. What is essential is that they put it into practice.			
Does your organization deal with a 'recognized trade union' which negotiates on behalf of its members with you?	If so, you will almost certainly have agreed Terms and Conditions of Employment for members with the union. Usually, this will provide a sound framework for handling grievance and disciplinary issues.			
Does your organization provide formal induction training for new employees?	This is a good opportunity to get new employees off 'on the right foot', knowing exactly what you offer to them as an employer and what you expect of them as employees.			
'Retrospective' induction	You should also think about 'retrospective' induction for existing employees missed for any reason, or who may have been inducted some time ago (the law and your requirements may both have 'moved on' since).			
Do you have an appraisal system or an equivalent system for agreeing objectives with employees and giving them objective feedback on their performance?	Fairly used, an appraisal system is an excellent way of managing employees, whatever their status. Records of appraisal interviews and achievements against agreed objectives should provide good evidence of fair, consistent management approaches.			
Have all employees been issued with a Contract of Employment and Written Terms and Conditions of Employment?	A legal requirement, to be issued within two months of an employee's date of starting work. Smaller organizations employing less than twenty people are exempt from this requirement. However, it is good practice to do so anyway – fairer to employees and evidence of your own good faith and desire to be a reasonable employer. You need to look at the situation if you take over an existing organization,			

Question	Notes	Yes/No	Action you will take	By Date
	in case the previous owners had not complied with the law.			
Has the Contract been based on, or 'cross-referenced' to, a model provided by, for example, your Trade Association, DTI leaflet PL 700 or the Chartered Institute of Personnel and Development?	Using a model document can save you time and ensure that you have access to the expertise and experience of organizations who work principally in the field of employment law.			
Do the Terms and Conditions include a formal Grievance Procedure?	To be seen as fair, the Procedure should state clearly: • with whom an employee should raise a grievance in the first instance • the appeal procedure that the employee should follow if not satisfied with the initial response.			
Do the Terms and Conditions include a formal Disciplinary Procedure?	A normal, fair Procedure will include a number of stages: • Informal Warning or admonishment (not recorded) • Formal Verbal Warning (recorded) • First Written Warning • Second (and/or Final Warning • Dismissal. It is prudent to keep a record in an employee's personal file of all warnings issued, with dates, and to require the employee to sign a copy to prove that (s)he is aware of the action taken. This includes 'verbal warnings' – if no written record is kept, how can you prove that it was issued?			
Do the Terms and Conditions state that an employee has the right to be accompanied by a colleague (or trade union representative if appropriate) in any disciplinary proceedings?	It is important, to be fair and seen to be fair, that the procedure is 'open' and that an employee cannot be pressured unduly by his or her boss 'behind closed doors'.			
Do the Disciplinary Procedures include provision for an 'improvement period'?	This relates to formal warnings. A reasonable period for a serious matter might be six months, after which the employee's performance will be re-assessed. 'Open-ended' warning periods will almost certainly be seen as unfair – you can't reasonably expect someone to work out a 'life sentence' for one offence.			

   REPRODUCED FROM *HOW TO AVOID EMPLOYMENT TRIBUNALS*, COLIN EVERSON, GOWER, ALDERSHOT

Question	Notes	Yes/No	Action you will take	By Date
Do the Terms and Conditions spell out what will be seen as 'Gross (Industrial) Misconduct'?	You do not have to predict every possible situation. Gross (Industrial) Misconduct offences specified will often include: • fighting, 'horseplay' and unruly behaviour – including verbal abuse of work colleagues • major breaches of Health, Safety and Hygiene (Legal or Organization Requirements) • refusal to obey any reasonable instruction – for example refusing to work with another employee because of their colour or gender • theft of, or malicious damage to, the organization's property • illegal trading /disclosing trade secrets to a competitor. This is not a comprehensive list – it is impossible to envisage every situation which might arise in every organization. Common sense still has a part to play in deciding what constitutes Gross Misconduct.			
Is it clear that Gross (Industrial) Misconduct will lead to 'Summary Dismissal'?	Summary Dismissal is a severe sanction, taking away benefits that may have accrued to an employee over a long period. It should only be used where the offence is so grave that (s)he must be removed from the organization instantly.			
Is it made clear that Summary Dismissal is Dismissal without Notice or any payment in lieu of notice?	It is fair and proper to ensure that employees know just what the penalty means – and what it will be imposed for – at the start of their employment with your organisation.			
Do the Terms and Conditions specify what sanctions other than dismissal may be imposed for breaches of discipline short of 'Gross Industrial Misconduct'?	These might include: • demotion • suspension (with or without pay) for specified periods • transfer to another department or site (away from the source of trouble) • specified 'fines' from wages (subject to any maximum legal limits in force) • Dismissal with Notice as set out in the Contract and subject to employment law.			

Question	Notes	Yes/No	Action you will take	By Date
Have you talked through these provisions with each employee individually, to ensure that they understand the rules by which they must abide?	It is good practice, and demonstrably fair, to take a little time to go through the rules – bearing in mind that some employees will have little experience of legally binding contracts.			
Has every employee signed a copy of their Contract which you have retained on their personal file?	This will be good evidence that you have issued the documents. The signature shows that the employee has had the chance to read them and query anything that they do not understand, or which they believe is unfair.			
Have any changes been made to the Terms and Conditions since the Contract was issued initially?	Changes should not be imposed without the consent of all employees affected.			
Have these been discussed with, and accepted by, the employee(s) affected?	If changes are imposed unilaterally, employees may have an action for damages or claim Constructive Dismissal before an employment tribunal.			
Do you use standard documents for issuing written warnings?	These can be very helpful, saving time and ensuring that you deal consistently with all employees across every department. Model documents are available from trade associations and organizations like ACAS.			
Do you always provide a 'written statement of reasons for dismissal'?	This is a legal obligation for employees dismissed after 26 weeks' employment. However, it is good practice to do so for any employee. Failure to do so may strengthen an employee's case if a claim is made to an employment tribunal .			

 REPRODUCED FROM *HOW TO AVOID EMPLOYMENT TRIBUNALS*, COLIN EVERSON, GOWER, ALDERSHOT

 **Appendix 3**

How to Handle Employment Tribunals: Personal Action List

Date Used:

Resource section	*Action you intend to take*	*By (specify date)*
How to use this resource		
Introduction		
The risk management approach to employment tribunals		
'Where there's blame, there lies a claim'		
Personal Attitude Questionnaire		
Case Study 1: Unfair Dismissal		
Case Study 2: Constructive Dismissal and Race Discrimination		
Case Study 3: Unfair Dismissal and Sex Discrimination		
Procedural checklist		
Tribunal procedures		
Glossary		